*The Canons of the Medieval Coptic Orthodox Church*

*The Canons of the Medieval Coptic Orthodox Church*

# THE CANONS OF THE MEDIEVAL COPTIC ORTHODOX CHURCH

Jonathan Adly

*The Canons of the Medieval Coptic Orthodox Church*

AGORA
UNIVERSITY
PRESS

**The Canons of the Medieval Coptic Orthodox Church**

Copyright © 2021 by Agora University Press

All rights reserved. Printed in the United States of America. No part of this book may be used or reproduced in any manner whatsoever without written permission except in the case of brief quotations embodied in critical articles or reviews.

For information contact : aupress@agora.ac
Agora University Press: press.agora.ac

ISBN 978-1-950831-40-1 (print)
      978-1-950831-41-8 (ebook)

HIS HOLINESS POPE TAWADROS II
118th Pope and Patriarch of the great city of Alexandria and the See of St. Mark

HIS HOLINESS PATRIARCH IGNATIUS APHREM II
Patriarch of Antioch and All the East

## The Canons of the Medieval Coptic Orthodox Church

Printed in the United States of America

*To Mariam, whose love carries me forward.*

*To Theodosius and Joy, who make my world a much better place.*

*To my dad, the best role model anyone could wish for.*

*To my mom, the first teacher I ever had.*

# Table of Contents

Acknowledgments.......................................................

Introduction..............................................................3

Chapter I
Two and a half and a quarter dirham         6
The Canons of Christodoulos                 11
After the Canons                            21

Chapter II
The Armenians                               27
Writing the Canons of Cyril                 33
The Canons Introduction                     39
The Canons of Cyril                         46
After the Canons                            64

Chapter III
The Son of Sanhut                           68
Gabriel Ibn Turayk                          72
The Canons of Gabriel                       77
Saif al-Islam                               93

Chapter IV
The Context of the Canons                   110

Bibliography.........................................................115

About the Author................................................ 117

*The Canons of the Medieval Coptic Orthodox Church*

# ACKNOWLEDGEMENTS

The journey toward writing this book started in November, 2017—I stumbled across several newly published historical studies that were both rewarding and humbling in revealing my shallow knowledge about the story of Copts. Over the course of that journey, I had the immense benefit of working with and learning from so many generous individuals and organizations, to all of which I owe a great debt that I can never repay. This book would have never come to light without their support and encouragement.

First, I would like to thank the editors of this book, the team at Coptic Voice. Coptic Voice is a nonprofit organization, of which I had the good fortune of being part of its inception and Board of Directors. As their mission states, they are dedicated to building global Coptic identity through community dialogue, education, and advocacy. They provided a platform to express a unique vision and perspective to tell the story and the history of the Copts. I am also deeply indebted to Marianne Melleka Boules, Executive Director at Coptic Voice who personally oversaw the editing of this work.

I am also truly grateful to Agora University, not only for believing in the idea of this book early on and agreeing to publish it, but also for their invaluable advice and professionalism. They have made this publication far less daunting than it once seemed to me. I am especially thankful for Mary Ghattas who led the process and encouraged the effort throughout the journey.

Furthermore, I owe many thanks to my father, who early on fostered a spirit of belonging and service. During my childhood, I witnessed how he poured his love, passion, and ideas into growing a Coptic orphanage in Egypt from a tiny room to a large, successful organization that made the world a much better place. It was he who first showed me what it meant to serve and lead. As for mother, she too fostered an intellectual curiosity that she hoped would lead to a stable, successful, and a quiet career as a professional, but ended up springing about a life full of ideas. I love them, I am proud of them, and proud to be their son.

I am most thankful, and truly blessed for my wife, Mariam, whose patience and support never ran out as I pursued this book among many other endeavors. Most of all, her unshakeable faith in me and my ideas is the rock and the foundation of this work. It has been quite a journey since I started this work, and she has been the only constant.

I dedicate this work to our daughter, Joy, who amazingly was always willing to hear me tell a story and Theodosius, our gift from God. They both inspired me to complete this work to the best of my ability.

# INTRODUCTION

s the eleventh century drew to a close, a Coptic deacon from Alexandria named Mawhub Ibn Mansur Ibn Mufarrij embarked on a mission to write the history of his people. He traveled throughout Egypt and its monasteries gathering the biographies of the sixty-five patriarchs before him. In the process, he translated their stories from Coptic to Arabic and wrote the biographies of two more Patriarchs whose reigns he personally witnessed, Christodoulos (AD 1046-1077) and Cyril II (AD 1078-1092).

His mission marked the start of a new age for the Copts; several, slow-moving but evolving trends coalesced to birth to the medieval Coptic Orthodox Church. Before Ibn Mansur, history was written in Coptic, but he and all who followed him wrote in Arabic. Similarly, the liturgical rites, theological treatises, and canons were all rewritten and expounded upon in Arabic. The heritage of that age lives to this day in modern Coptic Church practices and traditions.

Before the promulgation of these canons, the canons of the Coptic Church mainly consisted of universal church canons such as The Apostolic Canons, decrees of the ecumenical councils, and the letters Athanasius and other fathers of the church; all of which were written in Greek and translated into Coptic. The linguistic loss of Greek *and* Coptic, combined with the social pressures of a church living in a political structure emphasizing Islamic canon as divine law meant that new canons were needed. As the Coptic Church evolved to deal with the new realities of living in the shadows of the Caliphate, many canonical problems and practical issues arose, necessitating the promulgation of these canons.

This book does not attempt to introduce the Copts to a modern audience or expand on the transition from Coptic/Greek to Arabic Egypt. Rather, it attempts to make the canons of the medieval Coptic Church during that transition accessible to the modern reader. These canons are important as they are practiced and upheld today, but extremely difficult to access for the vast majority of readers. This book also attempts to explain the context and the circumstances of their promulgation. Simply stated, the goal of this book is to make the canons accessible to a modern audience and explore the reasoning behind each canon.

The last attempt to introduce the canons to a primarily western audience was done between 1932-1936, in a series of academic papers in *Le Muséon: Revue d'Études Orientales* (*The Muséon: Journal of Oriental Studies*). This book brings those papers together in one place, offers a fresh translation, and adds to the context and social circumstances of their promulgation based on a new understanding of *The History of the Patriarchs* as a primary source.

For the Coptic reader, the canons of the medieval Coptic Church serve as the basis for many of the practices and traditions of the modern Coptic Church and explains the origin of these practices. You will find these canons range from separating men and women during liturgical services to the specifics of fasting to the dates and practices of major and minor feasts. While this book is not meant to be edifying in the spiritual sense, I do believe it is historically and practically illuminating.

# CHAPTER I

## Part 1: Two and a half and a quarter dirham [1]

---

[1] Dirham is a silver coin, much lower in value than the prestigious golden Dinar.

C

hristodoulos, the sixty-sixth Patriarch of the Coptic Church, was ordained in AD 1046. He was a consensus pick after the failure of the nomination of an experienced administrator and a scholar, John Ibn Tirus. As the head of the Enaton monastery in Western Alexandria, John was the spiritual father of a powerful government official, and as such, many felt that he was bound to accumulate too much power in his office. Christodoulos was nominated in his place to ensure that John could not use the state apparatus to enforce his will.

Christodoulos, on the other hand, was a simple monk, with no government connections or wealth to his name. On the day of his ordination, all his possessions amounted to two and a half and a quarter dirham, an insignificant sum of money. He was pious, smart, and possessed a natural ability to understand other people and most importantly, himself. History immortalizes him as a gifted, self-aware leader. To illustrate, when a group of bishops came to ordain him, he refused to go with them unless they ordained him on the spot in his monastic cell. The point was to avoid going to Cairo or Alexandria, where he could easily get in the middle of a political game of concession and promises before his ordination to the office.

His patriarchal reign commenced well, as he was an eager diplomat, masterfully playing the role of a peacemaker among opposing factions within the Coptic Church. When a lowly deacon decided to omit the patriarch's name from the liturgy on his own, Christodoulos ignored the slight and eventually managed to personally win the deacon over.

Similarly, in his relationship with the government he avoided conflict as best as possible, even in instances where protest might have been justified. For example, early in his reign, the twenty-something nephew of a bishop named Phoebammon converted to Islam for unknown reasons. Only a couple of years later, Phoebammon changed his mind and wanted to go back to Christianity: an act of apostasy punishable by death. Christodoulos declined to intervene and the case arrived at its natural conclusion with the convert's death by the hands of an angry mob permitted by the local governor. No attempt is recorded by Christodoulos to save or hide the convert.

Nonetheless, to the Patriarch's credit after Phoebammon's death, he was given the treatment of a saint and a martyr with Christodoulos going as far as digging his corpse out from the original grave to be buried in a shrine inside a major church in Cairo.

Within the church, Christodoulos had several long-simmering issues that needed to be dealt with. First was the issue of simony, the practice of buying and selling ecclesiastical offices and clerical roles. Simony was common and practiced openly for a generation before Christodoulos. Many bishops, ordained by paying a significant sum of money, saw simony as their primary means of income and a way to recoup their original investment. Similarly, the same bishops were becoming increasingly independent and resisted any patriarchal involvement in their diocese. This state of affairs offers an explanation as to why Christodoulos, a simple monk, was chosen over the powerful and well-connected John Ibn Tirus. Little did these bishops know that Christodoulos, through a combination of persistent diplomacy and a lengthy thirty one-year reign, would be a powerful force of reform.

Very early on in his patriarchate, a serious attempt was made to depose him on the flimsy ground that he was not canonically ordained. His ordination happened in his monastic *cell* and not a *church*. While the details of the attempted coup are unknown, the names of the bishops who led it are recorded. Among them was Michael, Bishop of Tinnis, a scholar and historian with a reputation for his anti-simony and anti-corruption stance. It is likely that the attempt to depose the Patriarch was meant as a political maneuver to force his hand to stop simony, as Christodoulos trod carefully and slowly, given his conflict-averse and diplomatic nature.

The attempt failed; Christodoulos was supported by a high Coptic government official who backed the Patriarch and intervened on his behalf to defuse the coup. As was the pattern, Christodoulos went out of his way to accommodate the aggrieved bishops and eventually managed to reconcile them. The next time another dispute took place, Michael, Bishop of Tinnis found himself on the Patriarch's side rather than the opposition.

In addition to writing the first Coptic Church cannons in Arabic, Christodoulos is known for officially moving the Coptic Patriarchate from Alexandria to Cairo. It proved a significant and symbolic move, although on the ground, it was a minor event that no one noticed. No patriarch lived in Alexandria since the city was sacked by Andalusian Muslim pirates in the ninth century AD.[2] By Christodoulos' patriarchate, the city had not housed a resident patriarch for close to 200 years.

Christodoulos penned his canons early on in his patriarchal career, specifically on August 8th, AD 1048, as he struggled to establish his authority and limit the independence of the bishops and the monasteries. It may have resulted from a dispute with a group of monks about his decision regarding the issue of whether the Eucharist should be kept overnight and be reused or not.[3] He, seeing that it

---

[2] Jonathan Adly, Episode 61: The Death of a City, *The History of the Copts Podcast*, podcast audio, July 7, 2019, https://podcasts.apple.com/np/podcast/episode-61-the-death-of-a-city/id1356004270?i=1000444009299.

[3] The dispute was over the celebration of the Liturgy of the Presanctified Gifts.

was subject to "decay, change, insects, and other things besides"[4] commanded that this practice be abolished, anathematizing any who should do it afterward. In response, the monks "rose up against the father, the patriarch, and they came to him with the iron keys, and they said to him, 'You are no better than the fathers who preceded you.'"[5] Their refusal to heed his direction was mostly a rejection of the patriarchal authority to settle theological disputes.[6]

This, among all the other long-simmering issues inside the church, necessitated the writing of the canons. And so, with the help of Bishop Michael of Tinnis (who eventually became the Patriarch's secretary), Christodoulos set out to put down in writing the rules of the Coptic Church. As one would expect, the canons were a combination of on-the-ground traditions, Christodoulos' own stance on certain issues, and old canons translated from Greek and Coptic into Arabic by Bishop

---

[4] Sawius Ibn al-Mukkafa', *History of the Patriarchs of the Egyptian Church* Volume 2, Part 3, A. S. Atiya, Y. Abd al-Masih, O.H.E.-KHS Burmester (eds., trans.), (Cairo: Publications de la Société d'Archéologie Copte, 1959), 262.

[5] *History of the Patriarchs*, Ibid.

[6] The two centers of power for the Church of Alexandria were the Patriarchate and the monasteries, with the latter informing the ranks of the former. To this day, the theology and practices of the Coptic Orthodox Church reflect this monastic heritage.

Michael. They reflect the social and moral context of Christodoulos world and the influence of existing in a rapidly Islamizing society, albeit with a high degree of religious diversity and tolerance under the late-Fatimid rule.

## Part 2. The Canons of Christodoulos, The Sixty-Sixth Patriarch of Alexandria

1. Male and female shall not be baptized in the same font, and no one shall enter the church, unless bareheaded and barefooted.
2. None of the faithful shall cover his Eucharist with bread before the dismissal.
3. The faithful shall be careful regarding the water with which they cover their Eucharist. Just three draughts, so that nothing of it (the water) shall fall on the ground, as it is equal to the Eucharist.
4. The faithful shall stand in the churches on Sundays and feast days with fear and trembling in the presence of (lit. between the hands of) God, His Name be exalted. With supplication, entreaty, and petition for the remission of sins and delivery from the snares of the enemy. Further, no one shall talk or converse at the time of the prayers and the liturgy, except on

these two subjects, and they are the subject of religion and of the readings, and the science and the interpretation thereof, wherein (is the) salvation of souls. They shall give ear to hear the precepts of the Lord—praise be to Him!—until the liturgy be finished. The women shall stand in their places with continence, and they shall not utter a word during the time of the prayers and the liturgies.

5. The women shall not mix with the men. And they shall not sit in the passages of the men, so as to look at those who enter and those who go out. Further, the women shall be submissive to their husbands, and attentive to their homes, so that they may be blessed with the blessing of their mother Sarah and Rebecca and Rachel.

6. The faithful shall practice asceticism and humility during the Fast of the Pure Forty Days (Lent) like our Lord and Savior Jesus Christ, glory be to him. There shall not be during it (Lent) any marriage at all, or contract of marriage, or a dismissal or anything in this matter.

7. On Good Friday, there shall not be any baptisms or burial prayers. During it,

asceticism is mandatory because it is a day for mourning and lamentations.

8. After the completion of the Liturgy on the Sunday of Olives [Palm Sunday] there shall be read the Gospel of the Intercessions for the Dead after the Pauline Epistle which is appointed for the dead, and after this, there shall be read over the assembly of the people the Absolution, because on Good Friday, it is not allowed to do either the Intercession or the Absolution or the funeral rites until the day of the Feast of Easter is completed.

9. The Liturgy of the Great Thursday shall be done in fear and awe and in silence, without kissing or handshaking. And the "ابرسفارين" (*prosverin*) shall not be said but instead, *mata voi* (?) without absolution in the beginning or the end. In the Liturgy of the Great Saturday, the Intercessions and the Absolution shall be read, but the kiss of peace shall not be given.

10. There shall not be performed during the Fifty [Days] either baptism or ordination (lit. laying of the hands).

11. There shall not be allowed on Sundays weeping or lamentation or

wailing-women, and it is not allowed to a Christian to do this or anything of it for the dead, except the Intercessions and the Eucharist and the prayer for the dead and alms in the measure he is able; that the Lord may have compassion on the souls of your dead, and that He may bless your lives and your goods and your homes and your children, and that He may bring back the travelers who are absent, and give peace in your time (lit. fix your times).

12. None of the bishops or the priests or the deacons who are strangers shall, if he enter the city of Alexandria, celebrate the liturgy in its churches or make the offering on its altars, and no one shall cause them to make the offering in them (the churches) or to minister at all.

13. The faithful shall observe the Fast of the Apostles, which is after Pentecost, in thanksgiving to God, that He granted to us in it the gift of the Holy Spirit. Fasting continuously until the fifth day of Abib (June 29$^{th}$), and then they shall celebrate the feast on it, as the custom.

14. However, if that day falls on a Wednesday, they shall celebrate the feast and they shall not break their fast until

the normal time in the days of fasting. If it is on a Friday, they shall not break their fast on it.

15. Likewise, the Fast of the Holy Nativity shall be from the Feast of St. Mena (Mar Mena) on the fifteenth day of Hatour (November 11th) to the twenty-ninth day of Kiahk (December 25th).[7]

16. If the feast of Nativity falls on Wednesday or Friday, they can break their fast in it and not fast on that day.

17. Likewise, the Feast of the Holy Epiphany on the eleventh of Tubah (January 20th), if it falls on a Wednesday or a Friday, let them break the fast on it, and they shall not fast at all.

18. But, if the tenth of Tubah was a Saturday or Sunday, there shall be no fasting on it. Instead, they shall fast on the Friday before it.

19. It is not allowed for any of the faithful to fast on a Saturday, except on one Saturday in the whole year, and this is the Great Saturday which is the end of the Fast.

---

[7] The accuracy of this note is questionable considering that the Gregorian Calendar starts in AD 1582, almost 600 years after Christodoulos' reign.

20. Fasting is obligatory on Wednesdays and Fridays throughout the year, except in the Fifty Days (following Easter).
21. It is not permitted for a deacon to be late for a service or abandon the ministry of his church, or be absent from it on the days on which there is the liturgy, except for necessity, or bodily sickness, or by a government decree.
22. It is not allowed for a priest, if he did not attend the liturgy from the beginning, to make the offering or even touch the Holy Body with his hands.
23. No priest shall leave the altar with the incense after reading the gospel into the midst of the people, but he shall incense with it around the altar up to the time which is known.
24. When an infant is baptized, let him be fasting until he has communion, but if he has drunk the milk of his mother or of another woman of the faithful, the Eucharist is not allowed to him, and Baptism is not allowed without communion.
25. It is not permitted for a woman to sleep[8] in the church whether in feasts or

---

[8] Literally, to pass the night.

Sunday nights, unless she is an elderly or a nun.

26. He who marries a Melkite woman, it is not possible for him to be crowned with us (in the Coptic Church), until he has put a condition on his wife that she shall not go to any churches but ours and they shall not baptize their children except under us.

27. If the senior deacons are absent from the ministry of their churches, and then come on festivals and desire to officiate, this is not allowed to them. Those who shall officiate are those who regularly attend, regardless of their rank.[9]

28. If any deacon or a layman opposed a priest, or had a conflict with him, or was angry with him.[10] He shall not go to another priest drawing close to his hand.[11] If he went to another church, he shall not draw close,[12] and if he did, both he and whoever gave him communion shall be suspended.

29. Whatsoever deacon or other person has complained about a priest, and departed

---

[9] Literally, their inferiors.
[10] Literally, anger between them.
[11] Literally, take communion from him.
[12] Literally, take communion.

from the judgement of the Church and sought aid from the Sultan or the judge, and has turned away from the priests and the Church to someone else, and thought which is not his by right, if he is a priest, let him be suspended from his office, and if he be a layman, let him be forbidden the Eucharist.

30. Deacons and those who are below them shall not oppose their priests and they shall not depart from their judgement, for they are the trustees of the Church of God, and whomever honors them and the Church, God honors him. And whoever insults them, God shall insult him.

31. We allow the faithful to make holy bread (*Korban*) in their homes, and carry them to the church, each according to his ability. There shall be to them a reward and a forgiveness according to the measure of their faithfulness. And let them (*Korban*) be prepared according to what is appointed by the usual custom; first, because this is an assistance to the church, and second, so as not to increase its expenses.

Glory be to God forever and ever! This was finished by the help of God the Exalted.

*Marginal note one:*

> "This Father was the sixty-sixth of the Patriarchs of Alexandria, and it is said that he promulgated these Canons on Sunday, the eighth of the month of Misri, in the year 764 of the Martyrs, in a church of Alexandria, the protected. He ordained on that day a priest and sixty-two deacons after the consecration of the church of Archangel Raphael and many churches."

*Marginal note two:*

*(addition by another bishop, Michael of Damietta, around 350 years later)*

"ON THE RINSING OF THE MOUTH WITH WATER AFTER THE EUCHARIST AND THE COVERING OF THE EUCHARIST WITH BEANS AND LUPINES.

Our Fathers established a law for us that we should guard the Eucharist and should take care of it, and that after we take communion, we should make certain that there does not remain any things of it in our mouths, and rinse our mouth with water as a precaution, so that there may not remain anything of it in our teeth, or that any trace of the Blood of Christ remain on our lips, or while speaking that any things of it appear with the saliva of our mouths. Let us do this out of care and zeal for the Body of the Lord Christ and His Blood and let us rinse our mouths and swallow what we rinse with, and repeat the rinsing three times.

As concerns with the issue of covering the Eucharist with beans and lupines, there were in Egypt people called Sabaeans (al-Saba). They prayed to the east, intending to pray to the Sun; however, mixing with the Christians and dressing the same manner. The Sabaeans did not eat anything that comes from a square root as beans and lupines, as such the Copts made it a practice to eat beans and lupines in their churches, so that the Sabaeans might be discovered at the time of eating them. So that, whomever does not eat beans or lupines, they drive out from the assembly of God."

## Part 3. After the Canons

Egypt found itself in a precarious political position when the canons were written in AD 1048. The infamous Caliph al-Hakim died a generation earlier, leaving the Caliphate in the hands of his sixteen-year-old son. He was a weak figure who died relatively quickly from the plague in AD 1036, and another child-caliph, Al-Mustansir Billah was his successor.

Both Caliphs were puppets; the first was controlled by al-Hakim's sister, Sitt al-Mulk, and then by a competent vizier[13] of Iraqi origin, named Ali bin Ahmad al-Jarjarai. Sitt al-Mulk and al-Jarjarai's regencies were peaceful and prosperous but quite eroding to the legitimacy of the office of the Caliph. No longer would a Caliph rule in person. Instead, they served as mere figureheads while powerful men competed for the office of the vizier as the true head of a vast empire.

To complicate matters, al-Jarjarai died in AD 1045, making the reign of Christodoulos a difficult one as men struggled to fill the vacuum of power. Warlords and mercenaries constantly fought in the streets of Cairo for the office of vizier; civil war and famine remained a looming threat over the city's head. The political situation finally stabilized by the arrival of a powerful Armenian warlord in

---

[13] A vizier is a high-ranking political advisor or minister in the Muslim world. The essential head of the government in the context of the Fatimid Caliphate.

AD 1074. Christodoulos did not get to see much of that stability, as he passed away only three years later in AD 1077. His patriarchal career was carried out under lifelong civil unrest, his passing marked his long 30-plus year reign as one of heartache and anguish.

During this troubled career, he witnessed the governmental decree ordering all churches closed in an attempt to extort 70,000 dinars from the Patriarchate in AD 1057. Ibn Mansour, a connected Alexandrian with an uncle close to the governor, saw the events as they played out and recorded the event. We are told that the governor of Alexandria, sympathetic to the Christians, told Ibn Mansour's uncle to protect and hide the church's property before closing them, as *The History of the Patriarchs* recounts:

> "This (is) the letter of the vizier al-Yazuri which has arrived concerning the closing of the churches and the seizure of all their property and a demand for ten thousand dinars from all the Christians of Alexandria. It is necessary that you should go at once and remove all that is in your churches in the way of vessels and vestments and such like things, so that you may behold afterward what

I shall do tomorrow, and this affair shall be kept secret."[14]

Even in Alexandria, the tolerant governor was replaced for a new one who "passed the night in the Church of the Saint George the Martyr inside the sanctuary with a beardless youth"[15] in a show of intentional desecration, subjugation, or at least disregard to the feelings of Christians.[16]

Eventually, Al-Yazuri—the vizier decreeing the closing of churches—was killed by Turkish warlords within a year, and the Churches were reopened after the collection of 2000 dinars by the Alexandrians and 6000 dinars by the Patriarchate.

Shortly after, a quick succession of a major earthquake in AD 1062 followed by a smallpox epidemic that killed "twenty-one thousand young people within less than a month,"[17] and a decade-long civil war between Turkish and Nubian army factions, decimated the population of Egypt.

While the cities were emptied of their garrisons due to the civil war, Bedouin tribes raided the Delta extensively, specifically identifying clergy and churches as easy targets. In one of these raids,

---

[14] *History of the Patriarchs* 2.3, 14.
[15] *History of the Patriarchs* 2.3, 275.
[16] The boy was probably one of his slaves.
[17] *History of the Patriarchs* 2.3, 290.

Christodoulos himself was captured, enslaved, and then tortured.

He was later sold to the highest bidder, which fortunately was a Coptic scribe from Cairo who bid 3000 dinars for the Patriarch, paying 1000 dinars on the spot and promising the rest in installments: money he did not have. Christodoulos, humiliated, traumatized, and wounded, went door-to-door in Alexandria to collect the rest of the money. Even Ibn Mansour, in a very uncharacteristic manner, tells us how he himself donated to help the Patriarch.

Christodoulos' reign was a struggle for survival. Despite his best intentions, Christodoulos could do little in terms of reform beyond the canons. Simony continued to live on. However, rather than treating it as a simple payment for ordination, the Patriarch would ask hopeful bishops to "loan" the patriarchate a lump sum. Once ordained, half of whatever revenue the bishop's diocese brought would go towards the "loan" while the other half went towards operating the diocese or to the bishop as income. Ibn Mansour provides us with a lively example: the bishop of Samanoud paid a thousand dinars at his ordination pretty openly and publicly as a loan to the Patriarchate. Then, when he took office, half of any revenue he collected from the people of Samanoud went to himself as a repayment for the loan while the other half went to the operation of the diocese and his income.

It was essentially the old way of doing things, but more in the spirit of the canons: organized and codified in writing. The change, like the canons, was accepted readily. Christodoulos was widely known as an honest, pious Patriarch who did not practice simony, helped by the fact that he lived simply and humbly, away from both Alexandria and Cairo in a small city in the Delta.

Just before Christodoulos died, the newly arrived Armenian warlord, Badr al-Jamali, was purging upper Egypt of rebellious Nubian troops. A governor in the middle of that conflict complained loudly at how the newly arrived Armenians treated Christians better than Muslims. And so, to prove a point, the Armenian general brought Christodoulous, a dying elderly man at this point, to Cairo and imprisoned him on false charges.

When the fighting was over and the rebellious troops subdued, Badr al Jamali, the Armenian warlord recalled that governor to Cairo and released the Patriarch from prison. He intended to execute the governor for his complaints that jeopardized the war effort. He first asked the Patriarch to decide on the governor's fate. Diplomatic and wise as expected, Christodoulos responded by saying, "We do not have the right according to our religion to kill nor to render evil for evil, but you are the sultan, and authority belongs to God and to you." Al-Jamali responded by executing the governor as he planned. Just a few months later, Christodoulos died peacefully after a long 31-year reign with leaving a legacy as the pope who took the first step to transform the Coptic Church.

# CHAPTER II

## Part 1: The Armenians

The arrival of Badr al-Jamali to Egypt was a significant moment in the development of the medieval Coptic Church Canons. He, a convert to Islam ended up the force behind the promulgation of the second canons of our series, the Canons of Cyril. After gathering all the bishops in Egypt and giving them "a severe speech which God pronounced through him, he commanded them to draw up for him a collection of Canons of religion, and to present it to him."[18] And so, we must formally introduce the Armenian vizier, Abu Najm Badr al-Jamali.

Badr was a freed slave from Armenia with an obscure background. Likely a Christian by origin, he was enslaved and sold to the ruler of Tripoli in his youth where he was converted, trained as a soldier, and freed to fight on behalf of his master.

In the army, he quickly distinguished himself as a career officer and worked his way up until he was appointed military governor to Damascus in AD 1063. In the following decade as chaos reigned in Egypt, Badr successfully suppressed several rebellions in Syria and survived with his reputation as a competent administrator intact and his abilities as an army commander enhanced. He gradually started recruiting other Armenians to serve as the core of his personal army, which reached 20,000 men at its peak.

---

[18] *History of the Patriarchs* 2.3, 337.

In Egypt, the decade-long civil war between the army factions reached its lowest point when the Turkish soldiers expelled the Nubians from Cairo and then proceeded to loot the Fatimids' treasury. Desperate, the weak Caliph reached out to Badr to come to Egypt and take charge. Badr heeded the call and left Syria for Egypt in the winter of AD 1072.

Arriving at Damietta in January AD 1073 with a personal army of 10,000 Armenians, he proceeded to subdue Egypt with great efficiency. In less than three years, Badr al-Jamali laid claim to Egypt and ruled as an absolute military dictator with an iron hand, initiating a long period of peace and giving life to the dying Fatimid empire.

Badr was ruthlessly efficient as a ruler with an affinity for the rule of law and a strategic understanding of the tenets of good governance. Quickly, he eliminated most of the old entrenched palace elite, encouraged Armenian migration to Egypt to replace them, and incentivized long-neglected agricultural cultivation as a consequence of civil war and incessant raids.

While Badr was nominally a Muslim, most of his soldiers and new immigrants were Miaphysite Christians with the same faith as the Copts. However, they came with their own clergy, culture, and traditions, and, in time, had their own bishops and churches. Though barring a few personal incidents, on the whole, the Copts and the Armenians would get along fine but stay mostly in their own separate worlds.

As such, it is not surprising that Badr took a keen interest in the affairs of the Coptic church. Not just as a factor in the success of the Armenian migration project, but perhaps more importantly as a diplomatic channel to keep the southern borders of Egypt peaceful. And for that, he needed the cooperation of the new Patriarch ordained after the death of Christodoulos: Cyril II, the sixty-seventh Patriarch of the Coptic Church.

When Christodoulos died, an assortment of bishops, important priests, and civil servants in Cairo assembled to pick the new Patriarch. After three months of negotiations, the choice lay on an obscure monk named George to be the next Patriarch, renamed Cyril upon his elevation.

It seems that the choice fell on him because of exhaustion rather than any side dealing or promises. It was a tough decade for everyone, and they were desperate for any signs of a fresh start. Cyril was likable, pious, and had no enemies; and so, he was readily accepted by all.

At his elevation, he tried his best to keep a low profile, even going so far as trying to avoid Cairo and stay in a rural village instead. Nonetheless, Badr refused and insisted that the

Patriarch stay in Cairo; he was to be an important piece of Badr's plans to keep his borders peaceful.

In Sudan, a dangerous combination of sheltering former soldiers driven out of Egypt by Badr, a rabid process of Islamization, plus a few political refugees from the old regime was brewing and threatening the stability of Egypt. And so, Badr needed two things in there. First, he needed to have eyes on the ground. Second, he needed the Ethiopians to serve as a counterbalance, an enemy to his enemies—given that Sudan laid in between Egypt and Ethiopia.

To achieve those two goals, he enlisted the assistance of the new Patriarch. A promising young monk named Severus was hand-picked by Badr al Jamali for his piety and learning to be the next bishop of Ethiopia. Then, once the choice was made, Cyril was told to ordain the young monk and make it official. And so—Severus became metropolitan of Ethiopia—but more akin to a modern ambassador speaking on behalf of Badr al Jamali and relaying messages to and from the government in Cairo.

Severus's appointment illustrates Badr's ruthless efficiency. Ethiopia already had a bishop- a self-appointed one- rather than one from the Coptic church. To ease the process for the new metropolitan, the Armenian general arranged for the kidnapping of the self-appointed bishop by a group of mercenaries in Sudan who brought the pretender bishop to Cairo where he was quickly and quietly beheaded.

And Severus, for his part, even with an understanding of his objectives in Ethiopia couldn't help but rock the boat. The Ethiopian king as well as many nobles had many wives and concubines. Severus made it a personal mission to end the practice which ruffled a lot of feathers including the king himself. He even went as far as requesting from Cyril to write a synodical letter explicitly banning the practice, but it was mostly ignored. It was too entrenched of a practice to go away that quickly.

Lastly, Cyril's reign was entirely free of simony. The previous decades had taught everyone a few harsh lessons and a new generation of clergy wanted nothing to do with it. This was no doubt helped by the prosperity of Badr's reign and the fact that many contributed willingly and generously to the Patriarchate with little resistance. That did not mean that his reign was trouble-free. Cyril had a problem that haunted him throughout his reign: his lack of formal education. As Ibn Mansour tells us, "He was, at the beginning, of little learning, like

Demetrius[19] the former father, but he was a good priest."[20]

If we read between the lines, it seems that he couldn't even read or write, which made him an easy target for manipulation. This played out in two ways. The first, early in his reign a group of bishops directly confronted him about how his retinue was putting decrees in writing under him without his knowledge and that he should dismiss them. However, he fought back trusting his lieutenants. After a tense back and forth, he ended up removing one of those lieutenants.

More seriously, his illiteracy caused him immense problems when dealing with Badr. Badr was truly an exceptional leader with an uncharacteristic zeal for the rule of law: actual, written, and codified rule of law. He, as a benevolent dictator could break that law, but no one else could. Not governors, not rich men, and definitely not Christian clergy or Muslim imams. And so, apparently tired from having to hear cases about clergy behavior and complicated marriage and inheritance issues, he decided to do something about it. He told Cyril to bring all the bishops that he could bring and come for a conference with him.

---

[19] Demetrius, known as the Vinedresser, was the 12th Patriarch of Alexandria (d. AD 232). He was thought of as an illiterate Patriarch in the Coptic tradition and is best known for his opposition of Origen (AD 184- 253).
[20] *History of the Patriarchs* 2.3, 333.

Out of fifty four dioceses, forty seven bishops attended the conference, which was quite impressive. There, Badr asked them to produce a definitive, canonical set of laws they must abide by. Rather than obscure theological issues like when and when not to fast, these laws should have specific instructions about marriage, inheritance, behavior of clergy, punishments for offenses, and so on. In essence, Badr tasked the clergy to create their own version of a Christian *Shari'a*.

Time would prove this as quite a difficult task. Not only was Christianity never meant to have a shari'a, but the Patriarch leading the effort was utterly unprepared for such a thing; Afterall, he was completely illiterate. The last thing Cyril wanted to do was to be part of that project, both philosophically and practically. Yet somehow, despite his opposition, he left us *The Canons of Cyril* as his legacy.

## Part 2. Writing the Canons of Cyril

The process of writing the canons of Cyril was quite chaotic and messy. As soon as the meeting with Badr ended, the attendees split into two factions. The first was a small group of 3 bishops, a deacon, and two laymen who were excited and passionate about the project. The second was everyone else, including the Patriarch Cyril. They were looking for any way to avoid granting the powerful Badr his wishes. The first group, the "adversaries of the Patriarch" as Ibn Mansour puts it, were also joined by a powerful government official named Joseph who was the superintendent of the personal holdings of Badr.

To be clear, Cyril and the bishops' opposition to the canons was not necessarily about the idea of writing cannons in principle, as Christodoulous' canons were just written a generation earlier. Rather, it was about Badr's intention to incorporate these canons as part of the state apparatus. In essence, once you put a canon explicitly dealing with the issues of inheritance and divorce down in writing, it was no longer the individual bishop or the Patriarch giving judgment on a case by case basis, but government agents. In short, they rejected the codifying of Christian principles into law.

Not to mention, there were a plethora of thorny issues where different regions of Egypt practiced different modalities and different monks and monasteries had different opinions. From issues fundamental to Christianity such as the practice of confession to more secular issues like how to handle the issue of concubines, cultural variances existed throughout. For example, the sacrament of confession would be an issue of major contention, all the way up to the thirteen century.

Openly opposing Badr with his iron hand and efficient ruthlessness was a fool's errand though, and as such, Cyril and the bishops needed to be circumspect about their approach. Rather than refuse the task outright, the plan was to slow the process down to a halt until Badr gave up or moved on.

However, their plan was foiled by the smaller group as they constantly wrote letters to Badr complaining about the Patriarch and his lack of enthusiasm about the canons. Furthermore, Joseph's closeness to Badr made sure that those letters arrived at their destination and were read.

Eventually, one of the folks in the Patriarch's circle confronted Joseph about these letters. Joseph, an important figure in his own right responded back harshly. The Patriarch had to intervene, but again, Joseph just heaped abuse on the Patriarch himself. However, Cyril did not respond in kind given his emotional intelligence and righteousness. Upon hearing Joseph's insults, he "descended from his beast, and he bowed down to him"—an act of humility common in monastic circles between elder and disciple. Followed up by an iconic "Joseph, if you have a sovereign of the earth, I have Christ the sovereign of heaven and earth."

The end result of that dynamic was that the vast majority of the Coptic bishops were excluded from the process of making those canons. Only the five men of the first group plus Joseph compiled and wrote them. Once they were finished, Cyril, not wanting to rock the boat or anger Badr gave their work his blessing by writing an introduction with a blessing. However, the damage was already done, and the canons immediately became irrelevant; a symbolic treatise that no one paid much attention to.

First, with little participation from the Coptic hierarchy, they possessed no legitimacy that Badr could use to judge among his Christian populace. Second, the small group writing the cannons were no law experts. Their excitement didn't make up for the fact that they probably had little formal education and didn't know how to address the many thorny issues of Medieval Copts. It is unlikely they dusted off the Codex Justinianus[21] or Augustine's works and went from there. Lastly, Joseph ended up in trouble with Badr for an unrelated matter, probably taking part in an attempted coup by Badr's son that failed. The Armenian general, known for his no-nonsense justice—beheaded him before the project ended. He was the government's lead man on the project, and so with his death, no one pushed the issue in the palace.

---

[21] Code of Justinian, Latin *Codex Justinianus*, formally *Corpus Juris Civilis* (Body of Civil Law), collections of laws and legal interpretations developed under the sponsorship of the Byzantine emperor Justinian I from AD 529 to 565 with Christian inspiration.

The end-product was a small collection of 34 cannons designed to be as generic as possible with a wide degree of interpretations. In the end, it did not fulfill any of Badr's objectives or address any civil issues. Instead, the canons merely restated agreed-upon traditions of the time; a sermon masquerading as law. Eventually, Badr gave up trying to work with the church hierarchy. He came to the conclusion that bringing in Armenian clergy would be extremely useful for his administration and better use of his time. So, he invited or at least allowed the Armenian Patriarch to settle in Egypt a year later and supported him financially and logistically giving him a few Melkite churches to operate.

We are told by Ibn Mansour that in June/July AD 1087, a ship arrived from Constantinople to Alexandria that had,

> "a young man (who came) with pomp and companions and pages. It was said concerning him that he (was) the patriarch of the Armenians, and his name (was) Gregory, and that he (was) the son of the sister of their former patriarch."[22]

According to Ibn Mansour, Copts were highly skeptical of the Armenian patriarch at his

---

[22] *History of the Patriarchs* 2.3, 344.

arrival. "A young man with pomp and companions" is not exactly how you would want a patriarch coming to your city to be described. Nonetheless, a few developments changed that skepticism quickly and turned his arrival into a warm reception.

First, Badr al Jamali made it clear that Gregory was going to stick around and that accepting him would be beneficial if one wished to keep his head attached to his body. Second, the Armenian Patriarch had the political savvy to take a Melkite church as his residence and headquarters instead of a Coptic one. This was welcome news to the Coptic Patriarchate, who were invited to share the space with the Armenians on special occasions.

Most importantly though, what really made Gregory truly accepted and well-received was his connection to monasticism in Egypt. He was supported by a saintly Armenian monk who had been in Egypt for a long time already, where the monk sang him praises across Egypt. Further, together, the Patriarch and the monk drove out a demon from a possessed Alexandrian which impressed the everyday Copts, at least in Alexandrian circles.

This was followed up with a meeting with Cyril—which resulted in

> "the agreement of the Copts and the Armenians and the Syrians and the

Ethiopians and the Nubians on the Orthodox, upright Faith on which the saintly, virtuous fathers agreed, and with which Nestorius and Leo and the Council of Chalcedon disagreed.[23]"

It is highly unlikely that anybody was there but the Armenians and the Copts—so, this should be taken as Cyril and Gregory shaking hands and agreeing to work together.

## Part 3. The Canons Introduction

From Cyril, a servant of Jesus Christ, who is by the grace of God and His incomprehensible and inscrutable decrees patriarch of the great city of Alexandria, Egypt, its provinces, Ethiopia, Nubia, and of the five western cities, to all the beloved brethren, the virtuous bishops—may God protect them by His strong Right Hand—and to all the beloved children, the priests and deacons, and the rest of the Christian Orthodox people who love God, peace, grace, and blessing descend upon you all, great and small, henceforth and forever and ever. Amen.

Now, since it was the judgment of God and His incomprehensible decrees which advanced me to this great service which I cannot accomplish, and to the obligations which I am unable to fulfill, I

---

[23] *History of the Patriarchs* 2.3, 346.

placed my trust in the mercy of God the Exalted who called my lowliness. I had confidence in His wisdom and in the excellence of His aid for those who trust in Him. I had the help of the prayers of the blessed, and I supplicated God in humility, blessed be His Name! To regard my humility and to aid my feebleness, who raises up the wretched from the earth and sets up the feeble from the dunghill to make him sit with the chiefs of His people (Ps. 113:7-8).

The magnitude of the matter terrified me, especially, when I considered the saying of Moses who is great among the prophets. When God chose him to guard His people, how he said: "I am of stuttering tongue and feeble of speech (Exod. 4:10), and his suffering thereby." Then Isaiah, the possessor of the great voice, when it was ordered to him to go as a messenger, he said: "I am a man of unclean lips (Isa. 6:5)." Again, Jeremiah who was elected from the womb, said: "I ask You, O Lord, to help me, for I know not how to speak, and I am young and despised (Jer. 1:6)." And Amos said: "I am a shepherd of flocks gleaning acorns (Amos 7:14)."

Though I am incapable of this matter, and I can't do this service, I placed all my hope in God and put my confidence in Him, and in accepting, I became the heir to a matter about which I am unable to utter. I accepted the great, magnificent and lofty gift which was bestowed upon me from among the gifts of the Holy Spirit, without merit, and without knowledge of understanding. Not by deeds was I advanced, but by the incomprehensible judgments and inscrutable decrees of the Lord Almighty. Thereupon, I resigned myself to the command of God the Exalted, and I relied upon His assistance, and I made as my aim the care for the affairs of the holy Church according to my ability and my confidence in God.

I asked the Lord who has chosen the ignorant of the world, the One who exalts the despised and raises up the powerless, who has delivered the good tidings of His pure Gospel to a people unlearned and of no high rank. He has chosen and elected them through His wisdom and bestowed upon them strength and aid for His service. And I humbly asked Him to aid me, the One who gives great things to whomsoever He wills, to lowly men, and nothing opposes His will.

And now I bend the bow of my heart, and I make a Christian obeisance (*matania*)[24] to you all. I beseech you to stretch out to me a helping hand to save me and yourselves, and to strengthen me by the bonds of Christian love, and to help me with your prayers and your supplications to God—praised be He!—that He may grant to me His

---

[24] The act of bowing down to the ground in humility; *proskynēsis* in Greek.

grace, and may open my mouth and loosen my tongue, as regards the teachings of the Church, that I may judge with equity and rectitude. That He may help me to establish His rights that are due to Him and to execute His evangelical commands, and that He may direct me to that which pleases Him, so that I may not deviate from His will, either to the right or to the left, and that He may grant peace to the Church which He has entrusted to me, and that He may preserve the flock which He has entrusted to me. That He may preserve tranquility and peace in the whole world, that we' may be guarded and preserved from every evil hurt, and from every sinful deed. That we may be preserved from all-devouring lions and rapacious wolves until the end of the world through the intercessions of her who makes great intercessions at all times, St. Mary, and of all the Saints, and of the great St. Mark the Evangelist, and of the three Abi (St.) Macariis. Amen.

Since I have begun this writing with the aforesaid introduction, I have been careful to explain what God the Exalted conferred upon us, and what He showed to us through His compassion and His deliverance of us. It is requisite for us to awaken from the sleep of neglectfulness and to know that God will not cut off our hope or His mercy from us, and that He is with us, as He promised, for He said: "I am with you until the end of the world." We raise up to the Exalted One thanksgiving and prayers with clean hands and humble hearts, for He has delivered us from temptation.

It is requisite that we should observe the commands which are incumbent upon us, as well as upon you, O virtuous brethren, and beloved, noble, and blessed children; for it is not from us that you receive them, nor do you obey our commands, but you obey the commands of the Lord Who is able to destroy soul and body together in the fire of hell. For we are only ministers of the word and interpreters[25] of the words of the Lord Christ and His superintendents, and you are the reasonable sheep for whom He gave His Blood and redeemed you at a great price.

Know, then, the value of this gift, and learn that you are sought out by Him secretly for your disobedience if you disobey. And by us openly. Similarly, if you obey, then you obey Him and submit to His commands, and it is He who will recompense you for this, and His blessing will descend upon you.

Avoid, O beloved of God, that which angers Him, and hasten to do that which pleases Him and leads to His mercy. For you have heard what Saint James says in the *Katholikon*,[26] when he says:

---

[25] Literarily, translators.
[26] The epistles written by disciples and apostles other than Paul.

"Faith without works is dead, and that the devils believe and tremble, and again that the strong man knows not when the thief comes to him, so let us be on our guard (James 2: 18-19, 26)."

I have set forth at the end of this epistle chapters containing the Canons[27] of God Whose power is great, and His commands, some of which (relate to) what has been reported to me, as having been neglected in part, while others that of which I wish to remind you with, by a Christian obeisance[28] for the sake of the Lord who is merciful unto us, you may save me and yourselves from the consequences of what I write to you.

Likewise you, O brethren, the bishops, may God preserve you with His strong Right Hand and help you to perform His commands, and by an obeisance, you may investigate thoroughly your dioceses without oppression, without caprice, without partiality, and without worldly motives. So that you may execute in them (the dioceses) that which is commanded by God the Exalted.

I have included most of these matters in this writing of mine, so that you may learn how to answer for all that you do in the Day of Judgment,

---

[27] Literally, doors.
[28] Literally, remind you with humility.

and for which you may, perhaps, have to answer in this world. You have heard what the Lord said by the mouth of Ezekiel the prophet when He said: "O son of man, I have made you a watchman unto your people: hear my words and bring them to them. If you warn the sinner to repent and to turn from his sin, and he repents, then that sinner shall live, and you shall deliver your soul. And if you neglect it (God's word), then that sinner shall die in his sin, and his blood will I require from your hands (Ezek. 3:17-19)." And you have heard what Moses the prophet said concerning Jacob Israel and what he did from watching by night over the sheep of his father-in-law, and how he said: "I was watching at night and exposed to its cold, and I was exposed to the violence of the heat of the day, so that watching became for me a habit."

These were inarticulate sheep, and this was only a prophecy and a reproof for us, who are shepherds of the articulate sheep. Likewise also the shepherds who were keeping watch over their sheep, the glory of the Lord shone upon them, and they were worthy that the angel spoke to them and gave them the glad tidings of the birth of our Lord Christ, and they beheld the angels, and they heard the celestial praising. This is the reward of the watchful shepherds.

As for those who are neglectful, Ezekiel has reminded them of that with which God has threatened them, in regards to punishment (Ezek. 34:2-10), and he has explained that which I do not wish to explain to you — God protects you from hearing it. And may He strengthen you and remain with you, as He promised, and may He bless you, so that you may hear the joyful voice which the good servant heard when He said to him: Come now, O good servant, faithful you have been over a few things, faithful you shall be over many, enter into the joy of thy Lord (Matt. 25:23). And if this good servant was faithful, then in contrast to him there is the neglectful and disobedient servant. And I have shown from chapters of the Canons that which is to be relied upon with the help of the Lord Christ to Whom be glory forever and ever. Amen.

## Part 4. The Canons of Cyril

Before going into the Canons, a brief note on the usage of some terms used in the canons:

- **Anathematize/Excommunicate:** Removes clergy or faithful entirely from the church; Unable to take communion. Considered to be the most severe consequence of violating a cannon. Literal translation: make unlawful.
- **Interdict**: Depending on the context, either prohibits communion or a specific act of ministry. Literal translation: prevent.
- **Suspend**: Suspends a clergyman from his office, but he is still allowed to receive Holy

Communion as a layman. Literal translation: cut off.

## The Canons of Cyril

*Canon one:*

- It has reached my humility that certain people (referring to bishops) seek a bribe for conferring the priesthood. Whosoever does this and accepts for the gift (of the priesthood) a bribe, or who promises a bribe, so as to bring this to pass by means of deceit and fraud, his authority shall not be accepted, and he shall not be accepted, and he shall not be to you other than in the condition of a heathen, and he shall be excommunicated, anathematized, and expelled from the Church of God, both he and the one who does it. And his company shall be avoided, as our father Peter avoided the company of Simon the sorcerer and expelled him from the Church of God at the command of the Holy Spirit, as it is said in the canons:[29]

- Let the chief instruct the people and let him bind them together by means of the Cross, not by anathema, and

---

[29] Unclear what canons are referred to here.

he shall not interdict or anathematize, except for a necessary reason. And if he anathematizes or interdicts anyone without a reason, seeking thereby to avenge himself upon people and craving for their humiliation and their submission, let him be the one who is interdicted and anathematized by God and His judgments, and they shall be innocent of this, and let his priests rise up against him with due reason. And if this is difficult for them, they shall carry his affair before his metropolitan or before his patriarch, since they rise up against him with due reason.

- And they shall not allow him to transgress against the sheep of Christ which He has redeemed by His immaculate Blood. And he (the bishop) shall not anger them, nor shall he force them to blaspheme against God and to deny His holy religion, and let the virtuous believer accept his (the bishop's) injustice towards him. And the canons[30] also said:

---

[30] Unclear what canons are being referred to here.

- He (the bishop) shall not be allowed to remain as a leader, nor shall he be close to leadership. (He) who is proud of heart and who is haughty and puffed up over the people, who considers that he is the most important of men, the most exalted of them, the most influential among them, and who regards the people of God with disdainful eyes. Rather it is he who is despised by God Who chastens; such one shall not be held in good esteem in his life, and the mercy of God shall not be upon him at his death, and he shall be deprived of his priesthood.

- And concerning this the Scripture says of God Whose praise is great: I will transform grace into its contrary for the proud.

### Canon two:

- Any bishop or priest who does not receive the repentance of a sinner, if he repent and return to God from his sins, shall be excommunicated from the Church of God, because he has opposed the saying of Christ which says: "There is great joy in Heaven on account of one sinner that repents" (Luke 15:7).

## Canon three:

- It is incumbent on every bishop to visit all his churches and his monasteries and to attend to their needs, and to their produce, and to their lands, and to all that belongs to them, and to the management in them, in the fear of God.
- The first expenditure from these (income of the diocese) shall be for the needs of the church, for making the Eucharistic bread (*Korban*), for incense, fuel, mats, and other things besides, that they (the churches and monasteries) may be firmly established, and may observe that which is pleasing to God.
- And he (the bishop) shall be attentive to their cleanliness, their organizations, and the performance of the prayers at the appointed and fixed hours. Whosoever opposes this law or neglects it is answerable to God the Exalted.

## Canon four:

- It is incumbent on every bishop to investigate the condition of his priests in the monasteries and the villages and to examine their affairs, as regards their behavior, and their liturgies, and what they undertake to do with regard to the reading from the five books at every liturgy, which are: the Pauline Epistle, the Catholicon, the Acts, the

Psalm, and the Gospel, and the prayer (*oushia*)[31] shall be read for each of these five books. He (the priest) shall not abridge anything of them; and he who abridges in his liturgy the reading of anything from these five books shall be anathematized by God—praised be He.

- The bishop shall advance towards them (the priests) with incense, and he shall instruct them in what is necessary for them, as regards desirable qualities, for they are examples to the faithful, and their chiefs. He shall advise them also in that they should be careful in bearing witness. When they bear witness, none of them shall give evidence about anything, except after knowing that it is correct. Whosoever opposes this, judgment shall be upon him according to what the circumstances warrant.

*Canon five:*

- It is likewise incumbent on the bishop to care for his priests and his people by means of godly teaching which will deliver both him and them from their sins; and for every soul of them (the priests and people) their shepherd is answerable, as has said St. Basil.

*Canon six:*

---

[31] Literally, litany. A prayer before each reading.

- It is not permitted to a bishop, or priest, or deacon, or layman to live with a woman at all, unless it is a mother, or a sister, or a paternal aunt, or a maternal aunt who are forbidden to him. Whosoever opposes this, judgment for disobedience is necessary for him.

*Canon seven:*

- It is incumbent on the bishop to visit those who are in his diocese, the priests, the sick, the orphans, and the widows, and to supply their needs and to establish for them that which is essential; otherwise, he is the same as a murderer of his brother.

*Canon eight:*

- It is incumbent on the bishop to not befriend any, except him who is honest in his manner of living and whose conduct is known to the chiefs of the monks or to the chiefs of the laity whose status is known, and to visit the superintendents of the churches. Whosoever finds him (the superintendent) unsuitable for the service of the church shall dismiss him, and shall employ him who can undertake the service, and who is honest in his manner of living.

*Canon nine:*

- It is requisite that none of the bishops should permit any of the monks to dwell in any part of his diocese, unless he (the monk) be in a monastery appointed for this, or he be appointed to the service of a church or for anything else. And he (the bishop) shall not permit him (the monk) to reside there, unless it be for some affair of which the bishop knows, and permits him to reside there for a few days, until he has accomplished his business and returns to his monastery. And if he stays after this, then the bishop shall interdict him, and forbid his (the monk's) company, until he returns to his monastery.

*Canon ten:*

- If any bishop or priest or deacon or other member of the orders of the Church or the ranks of the Orthodox laity transgresses against the law and acts contrary to the rules of the Church, so as to cause a tumult or (does) anything in the matter of his rite without the permission of the bishop shall be interdicted.

*Canon eleven:*

- It is requisite that the priests and the laity should not undertake any worldly matter on a Sunday, whether it is selling or buying, and they shall not be occupied with any work on it (Sunday). Rather, they shall be diligent in attending the church, the prayers, and the Eucharists. None of them shall talk at the time of the liturgies until they have received Communion. He who observes this, the Lord — praised be He! — shall bless him.

*Canon twelve:*

- It is incumbent on all the priests and the laity, that if a dispute or any worldly matter arise between them, to guard against any of them going to any other legal authority than that of the Church, but they shall go to their bishop that he may judge between them, and they shall not go away to other legal authority, except at his command.

*Canon thirteen:*

- The bread of the Eucharist (*Korban*) must not be baked, except in the oven of the church, nor must a woman knead it. Whosoever transgresses in this shall be anathematized, and every priest who learns of it and does not report his case to his bishop is a participant with him in the sin.[32]

*Canon fourteen:*

---

[32] This canon contradicts Christodoulous' 31$^{st}$ canon that permits the preparation of the Eucharist at home.

- It is incumbent on all Christians to fast during the pure Forty Days (the Great Fast), and at the Fasts of the Apostles and the Nativity at their seasons, and on Wednesday and Friday throughout the whole year, except during the Fifty Days alone.
- Whosoever observes this and performs it, the Lord shall bless him and forgive him his sins. Whosoever opposes it, if he be a priest, he shall be warned that he may conform, otherwise, he shall be excommunicated, and if he be a layman, he shall be forbidden the Eucharist. Whosoever of the priests learns of this and communicates him shall be interdicted, unless he (the communicant) be a child under the age of puberty, or a sick youth who has an evident excuse for exempting him from fasting.

*Canon fifteen:*

- It is incumbent on bishops to be circumspect in concluding marriage contracts, and none of the priests of the Church shall conclude a marriage contract until after they have fully examined the man and the woman, and they know for certain their condition, and that there is not any deception or anything suspicious about either of them. And he (the priest) shall make certain of their names, and of what has been agreed upon between them in the marriage contract with regards to the amount of the dowry and the period between the crowning and the marriage. Further a woman shall not marry until after her puberty. Whosoever opposes this shall be interdicted, and likewise the priests of every village shall conform to this.

*Canon sixteen:*

- It is incumbent on all the priests and the laity to honor the bishop and to respect him and to acknowledge his right. Whosoever transgresses in this and does not recognize that he (the bishop) is one in whom God has placed His trust, and states anything untrue about him, or vilifies him, opposes God, because He has said: You shall not speak evil of the ruler of your people.

*Canon seventeen:*

- It is requisite that the laity also guard against this (speaking evil of their bishop), and they shall honor the priest and the deacon in like manner.

*Canon eighteen:*

- It is incumbent on the faithful during the Holy Fast to guard against the use of any food that they use at the times of non-fasting, and none of them shall transgress even to the eating of fish and the drinking of wine, that their fast may be holy and perfect.

*Canon nineteen:*

- It is incumbent on all the faithful who choose to circumcise their children that they should circumcise them, if they choose (to do so), before baptism. It is not permitted to any of them to circumcise his child after baptism. Whosoever transgresses (in this) and does it, shall be interdicted and shall have no portion with us.

*Canon twenty:*

- If a Christian has a wife and marries another woman during her (the wife's) lifetime and cohabits with both the women without having a reason for leaving the first woman, shall be interdicted and anathematized.
- As well as every priest who learns of this and communicates with him (the man), before he has separated himself from the second woman and has returned to the first woman and has made manifest his repentance and is forgiven by the bishop.
- if he (the man who marries another woman) is a priest he shall be excommunicated and there shall be no repentance for him.

*Canon twenty-one:*

- If a Christian takes a concubine in addition to his wife there shall be no absolution if he continues in this (sin). And if he continues in it, after hearing this saying, he shall be excluded, and he shall have no authority to enter the church, and he shall not receive the Eucharist until he has separated himself from the concubine and returned to his wife. If a priest communicates him, after he learns of this, he shall be excommunicated and shall be a participant with him in the sin.

*Canon twenty-two:*

- If a Christian has a wife and deserts her and marries another woman without the excuse of adultery, and receives from the second woman a child and makes his child a pretext for not separating from the second woman, still, he shall not be permitted to dwell with the second woman; but shall be excluded and have no authority to enter the church, and he shall not receive the Eucharist until after his separation from the second woman and his return to the first woman.
- If he refuses, he shall be anathematized, and every priest who learns of it and communicates with him shall be anathematized and interdicted together with him.

*Canon twenty-three:*

- If a man has concubines and is not married, he shall not receive absolution if he remains with any of them; but he shall restrict himself to only one of them whom he desires, or apart from them, to another woman of the faithful, and he shall marry her according to the law, and he shall send away the rest (of the concubines). Whosoever opposes this and continues as he was, after having heard this sentence, shall be anathematized. Every priest who learns of this and who communicates with him (the man) shall be anathematized, and he is a participant with him in the sin.

*Canon twenty-four:*

- It is incumbent on every Christian to show love for his wife and to be a partner with her in all that is pleasing to God the Exalted, for she is his wife and his body, for she was taken from him, and to fear God in dwelling together with her.
- And it is incumbent on the married women of the faithful to offer obedience to their husbands and to submit to their commands, and they shall not oppose them even in prayer or vow because it (the prayer or vow) shall not be accepted from a woman, except with the permission of her husband, because

God has preferred him to her. Whosoever opposes this, let him be interdicted.

*Canon twenty-five:*

- It is requisite that the women of the faithful should not dye themselves with henna, and, if a misfortune should befall one of them, they should guard against blackening their faces, or summoning hired female mourners and lamenting women. Whosoever does this shall be anathematized, and the priest who communicates him shall be anathematized, for he is a participant with him in the sin, if he learns of it.

*Canon twenty-six:*

- If a woman betrays her husband and deliberately does what God the Exalted abhors, and prefers to be separate from him (the husband), and refuses to have copulation with him, she shall be anathematized.

*Canon twenty-seven:*

- It is incumbent on all the faithful, if they make merry with wine, and there be present musicians and jesters, to guard against bringing any of them into the church. Whosoever transgresses in this is disobedient.

*Canon twenty-eight:*

- It is requisite that the women of the faithful should not be allowed to pass the night in the churches on the eve of a festival or on another occasion, and they shall not enter the church, except to hear the prayers, and to receive the Eucharist with quietness, modesty, and the fear of God the Exalted. Whosoever opposes this shall be interdicted, and so also every one of the servants of the holy church who had helped them (the women).

*Canon twenty-nine:*

- It is incumbent on all the faithful, both priests and laity, to guard against having communications with a priest who is interdicted or with a layman who is interdicted or praying with them. Whosoever does this and opposes, is a participant with him (the interdicted person) in the iniquity.

*Canon thirty:*

- It is incumbent on all the faithful to guard against selling one of their slaves to those who are not of the faith. Whosoever transgresses in this, let him be anathematized.

*Canon thirty-one:*

- It is incumbent on all the faithful, both priests and laity, to guard against habitual intoxication (with wine), disobedience, and devotion to vice, and they shall abstain from these things. He who continues in this, if he be a priest, he shall be excommunicated, and if he be a layman, he shall be expelled (from the church).

*Canon thirty-two:*

- It is requisite for the priests of the churches and for their superintendents to guard against soliciting anything from any of the faithful under the heading of charges for burial or baptism or crowning, unless the believer give this as a gift of his own accord, desiring thereby to gain forgiveness, for this is not forbidden.

*Canon thirty-three:*

- It is incumbent on the children of baptism to honor the holy altar and pure sanctuary and to prevent altogether the laity from going into the altars.
- The priests and the laity shall not enter the church, except they be barefooted and bareheaded, and they shall not stand at the prayer of the liturgies, except in this manner. None of the laity shall communicate until he has removed his turban from his head, and a

priest shall not go up to the Communion above the altar step, unless he has on a *sticharion*.[33] And he who is without a *sticharion* shall communicate away from the altar. He shall not eat or drink in the sanctuary nor shall he cover his Eucharist at the altar, except in a place apart, if he finds sufficient space, and if he finds not (sufficient space), let him go away from the altar.

### Canon thirty-four:

- These (are) the canons which we have restricted ourselves to mentioning, with a view to omitting long-windedness, and for a Christian obeisance. Let whosoever has any of these bad qualities abandon them and deliver his soul from iniquity, and the Lord shall bless him, and cause you all to be a just people doing that which is pleasing to the Lord, as said the Apostle Paul: "I desire you to be zealous in performing good works and to abstain from evil, so that you may fear God Whose power is great, and fear to stand before His Judgment Seat." Guard against hearing the fearful Voice, saying to those standing on His left: Depart from me, workers of iniquity, into everlasting fire prepared for the devil and his hosts; and of

---

[33] Literally, liturgical vestments.

God Whose power is great, I earnestly desire that He cause you not to hear this awful and fearful Voice, but that He may help you to obey Him and to do that which is pleasing to Him, that He may strengthen among you spiritual love and Christian brotherhood in which is the fulfillment of religion, and that He may forgive you your sins and pardon your faults and have mercy upon your dead and save your chiefs and grant to your children to live chastely and grant to you perfect happiness in the Kingdom of Heaven, and the eternal habitation, and the paradise of delights after long years and a pleasant life through the intercessions of the Mistress, the Possessor of intercessions, the Mine of purity and blessings, Mary the Virgin, and[34] of all the Martyrs and Saints. Amen. Amen. Amen. Glory be to God forever and ever.

## Part 5. After the Canons

Pope Cyril II died in AD 1092, two years before the death of Badr al Jamali. His reign was quite prosperous and stable, although with a

---

[34] To be accurate, geographically medieval "Cairo" was really the palace district of a complex consisting of Misr-Fustat-Cairo—a complex that eventually evolved into a large city, roughly equivalent to modern Cairo. For brevity, the complex is referred to as simply "Cairo."

few significant developments. First, Egypt now had two Patriarchs: one for the Copts and one for the Armenians, who held much more influence within the court of the vizier. Second, Christodoulous changed the Patriarchal seat from Alexandria to Cairo. Now, while the Patriarch was still considered the Bishop of Alexandria, he really conducted all of his operations as the Bishop of Cairo. Yet Cairo already had a bishop: a powerful power broker named Sanhut whom Cyril never really challenged.

As one would expect, Sanhut was quite anxious about the next patriarch and the dynamic of having to share Cairo with him. So, despite the Alexandrian clergy and elite's wishes to pick the Patriarch who in the name would be their bishop, they had almost no actual stake in the matter since he was not going to be operating in the city. On the other hand, the bishop of Cairo had a lot to lose or gain depending on the choice; but on paper, his opinions were just that—an opinion of one man who could only do so much to influence the election process.

Unable to get his pick, Sanhut went on a campaign to delay and block all candidates presented by the Alexandrians—until they gave up and went home for the winter to reconvene again in the spring. After a year-long oppositional campaign, Sanhut proposed a compromise that ensured his position in Cairo would be secure.

The compromise was to draft a document akin to a wish list by all of the stakeholders and then present that wish list to the next candidate nominated. If he agreed to abide by it, his nomination could go through and the process can conclude with everyone happy. If he did not then, the search would continue.

The document drafted by the group ended up including what you would expect. A ban against simony, providing a yearly stipend to the churches and the clergy in Alexandria and other mandates of that nature. But it also had a very important new item about the Patriarch and the Cairo diocese. To quote the document directly, the wish list stated:

> "you must return to the bishops of the Sees that which those who were before you, forcibly took from among their churches and their monasteries, and became sharers with them in their Sees."[35]

---

[35] *History of the Patriarchs* 2.3, 383.

Essentially, Sanhut wanted the Patriarch to go somewhere else and leave Cairo to him, an ambitious and an unrealistic request given how important Cairo was to the administration of the church.

The first nominee considered after the drafting of the document was a monk named Michael, a larger-than-life figure in the mold of Badr al Jamali. Michael was a Patriarch who inspired "awe and fear"[36] in his clergy and had personality with such force that "none of the bishops or the archons [were]able to resist him in speech or oppose him."[37]

With pressure from Sanhut, he preceded to sign the document, followed by his ordination to the Patriarchate in October, AD 1092. Within days- essentially as soon as Michael set foot in Cairo and realized the full extent of what he had signed – he became disenchanted with Sanhut. If he were to do his job in any realistic way, he had to operate from Cairo and take charge of the churches there; the days of Alexandria were long gone.

As such, he refused to acknowledge the document, fought and then banished Sanhut to al Fayoum, and essentially took control of Cairo. However, Sanhut had supporters who opposed the Patriarch's treatment of Sanhut and threatened to

---

[36] *History of the Patriarchs* 2.3, 386.
[37] *History of the Patriarchs* 2.3, Ibid.

escalate the issue to the Muslim administration – still Badr at this point. But Michael kept a firm hand on the patriarchate. For ten years, the patriarch would bring Sanhut back to Cairo whenever complaints got too loud and banished him once things cooled down, until finally excommunicating him altogether.

Sanhut's excommunication was supposed to be a part of a bigger plan to officially and permanently abolish the Diocese of Cairo altogether. But as fate would have it, shortly after the excommunication, Michael caught an illness and died. With this death, Michael could no longer enact his plan, essentially giving room to the partisans to return Sanhut to Cairo and claim divine justice as the cause of death for Michael.

A mere three years later, Jerusalem fell to Western knights who came in an armed pilgrimage that would come to be known as the First Crusade. The onslaught of a holy war meant, new realities, and new realities meant new perspectives in the Coptic patriarchs' position in Egypt and the role they would play in the Levant.

# Chapter III
## Part I. The Son of Sanhut

ith the passing of Cyril II, the narrative of the deacon Ibn Mansour ends. Picking up the narrative after him is an influential civil official named Ibn

al-Qulzumi, who took a significant step on our path to a fully formed Arabic-speaking church. While Ibn Mansour was likely bilingual, translating Coptic history and adding his own in Arabic, Ibn al-Qulzumi wrote exclusively in Arabic. Additionally, as a government bureaucrat, his Arabic was flawless and flowery. He was "an accomplished Arabic stylist and very much a citizen of the practical world of secular and ecclesiastical politics."[38]

He tells us, how after Michael's death, the Patriarchate remained unoccupied for a whole year while Sanhut campaigned unsuccessfully on his son's[39] behalf for the office. This finally ended when the Coptic civil elite in Cairo took charge of the process away from the bishops and pushed for the nomination of an elderly monk named Macarius. Ultimately, Macarius proved to be a weak figure who ended up completely sidelined and pushed away from Cairo to live in isolation in a monastery. Meanwhile, Sanhut and Gregory the Armenian Patriarch represented the Christians in Cairo.

---

[38] Mark N. Swanson, *The Coptic Papacy in Islamic Egypt (641-1517)*, (Cairo: American University at Cairo Press, 2010), 66.

[39] Likely biological by the description of a "young man," although he may have been a spiritual son. Although Coptic Orthodox bishops are celibate today, clerical family traditions were much less clear-cut and more complicated in the eleventh century.

Medieval patriarchal elections, especially in the late Fatimid period were an unorganized affair where the civil elite, the clergy of Alexandria, and the bishops competed to elect a patriarch to represent their interest. Macarius may have been picked as he was a benign figure with limited resources to interfere with increasingly powerful civil elite.

Macarius was still serving in isolation when Sanhut died in AD 1117. At first, Macarius aimed to abstain from ordaining a bishop for the diocese so that he could eventually return, but ultimately failed in his endeavor. In a lengthy exchange of letters in beautiful, almost poetic Arabic between the Patriarch and the Cairene elite the patriarch diplomatically tried to avoid direct confrontation through deflection and delay. Regardless, they kept pushing him to ordain someone. Finally, as a last-ditch effort, the patriarch told them to pick their own bishop and that he would ordain him if he proved to be suitable. Fearing this offer as just another delay tactic, the Cairene elite proposed a multi-step process of fielding candidates, 12 in total, then narrowing them down to 4 by consensus among the elite and finally—via a lottery pick following a divine liturgy-made their choice. Perhaps unsurprisingly, it was none other than John, the son of Sanhut, a patriarchal candidate only a few years earlier.

Now, there are a couple of thorny issues with the narrative of al-Quluzumi and the rise of John as a de facto replacement of the Patriarch.

First, is the reliability of Ibn al-Quluzmi's account. He was in the very heart of the Cairo elite and clearly a partisan of Sanhut and a protector of his legacy. He may have written his entire account to preserve that legacy. So, whether John was truly picked from a random lottery or if the process was truly transparent as he described is questionable at best.

The facts were, from the twelve candidates for the office, John was the only one who was neither a monk nor a priest. Also, he was the only one that was a part of the Cairo elite: an insider as opposed to a monk or a priest coming from a faraway place.

Additionally, the hand of a certain Abu al Fadl, a powerful Copt and the secretary of the vizier of Egypt (Badr's son—al-Afdal at this point), was clearly visible in the process. Gregory, the Patriarch of the Armenians, had to give his blessing before John was to be ordained. He did so at the behest of Abu al-Fadl who seemed to have been comfortably in charge of the whole process. He brought John to stay in his house, then took him to Gregory, and then ultimately decided on when and how he would be ordained.

Further, the ordination itself seems to have been a sensitive matter as care had to be taken because, as Ibn al-Quluzumi tells us:

> "they were afraid of the common people, lest there might happen to them some insolence from them on the way."[40]

Even the ordination itself was not performed by Macarius, but by three bishops brought by al-Fadl. When it was all done and finished, Abu al-Fadl made sure that John and the diocese of Cairo did not forward any of its revenue to the Patriarchate as was expected from the other diocese. Essentially, Macarius was persona non grata in Cairo. Abu al-Fadl was in charge there and more or less appointed John with the support of Ibn Quluzumi and the rest of his colleagues, likely without a wide support from the common people. Despite a long twenty-six year reign, the 69th Patriarch of Alexandria Macarius never managed to assert himself as the leader of the Coptic church.

When he died in AD 1128, life went on. He was not replaced, nor was there any attempt to field candidates for the office. John, son of Sanhut stayed in charge in Cairo as the acting patriarch alongside

---

[40] Sawirus Ibn al-Mukaffa', *The History of the Patriarchs of the Egyptian Church* Volume 3, Part 1, A. Khater and O.H.E.-KHS Burmester (eds.,trans.), (Cairo: Publications de la Société d'Archéologie Copte, 1968), 33.

Gregory, the Patriarch of the Armenians. Only when a crisis hit three years later in AD 1131 that the Coptic elite in Cairo decided to finally ordain a Patriarch. They appointed Gabriel Ibn Turayk, who wrote the last of our series of canons: *The Canons of Gabriel*.

## Part 2. Gabriel Ibn Turayk

The Patriarch Gabriel was unlike most Coptic Patriarchs in medieval Egypt. As a layman from the class of Coptic administrators that ran the government, the patriarch's reign marked a significant departure from his predecessors with a streak of significant reforms and a flurry of significant achievements. The new Patriarch Gabriel Ibn Turayk, or "Abu 'Ala" before his ordination, started his career working in the ministry of correspondence and then eventually as part of the staff of the treasury. As such, he was both an experienced administrator and highly educated. He was possibly fluent in multiple languages- or at the very least fluent in Arabic and Coptic- given his work in the ministry of correspondence. Further, he had an excellent reputation in Cairo as a pious and a generous man.

He was brought in the middle of a severe political crisis, as John, son of Sanhut was nearing the end of his life and probably disabled by old age. First, the vizier al-Afdal (Badr's son) was assassinated, which led to a period of civil unrest where the Caliph wrestled with powerful men over the control of Egypt. This was combined by an unrelenting territorial expansion by the Crusader states, constantly chipping away the Fatimid territories in Syria and Palestine. As the regime was collapsing under its own weight, internally with unrest and externally with more losses to the Crusaders, tensions and hostilities against the Christians began to simmer. We are told by Muslim sources how the Caliph (Al-Amir bi-Ahkam Allah) appointed a former monk, a certain Ibn Qusa to head the treasury. Ibn Qusa, either out of the worsening economic situation or because he was corrupt - or both- began a campaign of wealth confiscation from the civil elite that made him extremely unpopular.

"A Thirteenth Apostle, Lord over the heads of government and the Church"—as his enemies liked to smear him sarcastically. Either way, whether he acted properly in the interest of the state or was a corrupt oligarch, his unpopularity among the elite combined with the fact that he was a Christian placed over Muslims—a precarious situation even in the best of times—meant he wouldn't survive for long. By AD 1129, the Caliph was threatened with a popular rebellion because of Ibn Qusa. So, the former monk and his two assistants were arrested. The latter were imprisoned, but Ibn Qusa was beaten to death with shoes, beheaded, with his corpse nailed to a plank, to float down the Nile to the sea.

One year later, the Caliph himself was assassinated plunging Egypt further into chaos with a succession crisis that eventually ended with a new branch of the family taking over with civil war, coups, and counter-coups lasting for an entire generation until the Fatimid dynasty was extinguished altogether by Salah el-Din in AD 1169.

In this world of civil unrest and instability, Gabriel was ordained as the 70th Patriarch of the Coptic Church in AD 1131. Given the losses to the Crusaders and the dwindling economic fortunes of the masses, Gabriel began his reign in the midst of increased hostility and tensions directed towards the Christians of Egypt. His ordination was an agreement between the civil elite of Cairo and the priests of Alexandria. Becoming a Patriarch without any consultation from the bishops or monks of the church caused him many problems during his tenure: especially in the beginning of his reign.

In his first visit as a Patriarch to the Monastery of St. Macarius, the biggest monastery of the time, he had to deal with hostile and skeptical monks. Presumably, when praying the liturgy, in the end before communion, he added a tiny part alluding to the body of Christ becoming "one with his Divinity," in line with standard Miaphysite

Christology but different to what the monks of St. Macarius were used to practicing. It was a new addition, a liturgical innovation as far as they were concerned. As such, they requested that Gabriel stop the practice, or they would not acknowledge him.

Comfortable in his theology however, Gabriel did not back down. Quite capable trotting in deep theological waters, he insisted on using the phrase and eventually convinced the monks to agree to saying "it became one of his divinity" but also adding "without confusion and without mingling"' to guard against another heresy where his divinity was swallowed by his humanity. The phrase ended up being a standard practice that is used to this day., Meanwhile, the state of Christian education in Egypt was non-existent and many clergy in upper Egypt refused to incorporate "without confusion and without mingling" into the liturgy. Gabriel, despite his energy and knowledge, was battling in many fronts, and this dispute was by far the least practical. So, he let the folks in upper Egypt continue their practice, until eventually they too adopted the phrase.

In that same visit to the Monastery of St. Macarius, he compiled the Lectionary for the Holy Week, which is used to this day, codified the process for the consecration of the Myron oil used in the sacrament of Confirmation, and forbade the interment of the dead inside the churches.

Over the course of his fourteen-year reign, he ended up writing at least three formal lists of canons as well as two liturgical books with several important practices that have become standard practice. Additionally, he may have had Arabic New Testament and Old Testament available for use, which was a first for the Coptic Church.[41]

In the canons, heavy emphasis was put on being able to read to officiate, as most priests by this point had no working competence of Coptic, yet memorized the liturgy and prayed it as a magical chant where neither they nor the congregation understood anything. Gabriel was a practical man where he encouraged the adoption of Arabic as a liturgical language, yet still instructed the priests to teach their children Coptic. In a letter to his priests, he wrote to them:

> "It is necessary that you also begin to teach the priesthood to your children at the outset of each day, before the Arabic [instruction];"[42]

---

[41] The Syrian and Melkite churches adopted Arabic much earlier than the Coptic Church.

[42] See O.H.E. Burmester, "The Canons of Gabriel Ibn Turaik, LXX Patriarch of Alexandria," *Le Muséon* 46 (1933): 43-54.

and:

> "Memorize the Doxology, the Prayer that our Lord Christ taught to his disciples, and the Holy Creed in the tongue that the people know and understand [Arabic]."[43]

Essentially, the Patriarch Gabriel had to navigate a tricky period of transition, hoping to preserve the Coptic language while simultaneously making sure that his flock could understand the tenets of Christianity through an Arabic translation.

The published canons list of Gabriel can be divided in three parts, A short list of instructions to the Alexandrian clergy, laws of inheritance, and a comprehensive and extensive canon list that was last published in Arabic in 1993 in two volumes. The latter is considered a major canon of the church and is outside the scope of this work.

## Part 3. The Canons of Gabriel

Note about the Canons: As mentioned in the previous section, Gabriel wrote at least three canons. This is the shortest of them, and the most accessible.

*A. Instructions to the Alexandrian clergy*

---

[43] Ibid.

## Introduction:

At my arrival[44] to the protected frontier city (Alexandria), where may God prolong the life of the beloved children, the orthodox, and the learned priests, and preserve their strength and their happiness, and may He bless them and theirs and their children, and accept the good prayers of my wretchedness for them, through the intercession of the Pure Lady, the Virgin, the Mother of the Savior, and the blessed Saint Mark the Evangelist, and all the Holy Saints. Amen. I wrote for them (the clergy of Alexandria) a number of canons that they might find support in them, and that they might act in conformity with them; and I have renewed for them in these pages the remembrance of them (previous canons) by means of short and abridged statements together with what has been added to them, that they may read them and abide by their contents, and they shall not depart from them. He who departs from the sentences of them (the canons) shall be suspended from the priesthood and he shall not have any power to act therein.

They are as follows:

### Cannon one:

- It is obligatory for the priests of every church to keep to their ranks and each of them shall serve the turn which is appointed

---

[44] Literally, the arrival of my humility.

to him each day. Each of them shall serve his day, and if it shall be weekly, both shall serve weekly; and if one of them be absent, the other shall take his place. If both of them are absent, then the office shall be (served) by him who is after them. And no one shall be absent from the church on the day of his liturgy, except with an evident excuse, and none of them shall bestow his rank on his son or on a near relative without the consent of him who is present with him (i.e., the congregation) as well as one who is higher than he is in the priesthood, because this raises discords and hatred. As for the Gospel of the Morning Prayer and the books and the diptychs, a near relative or a son can read them, or another.

*Cannon two:*

- The Liturgy shall not be celebrated until after there have been read the Apostles (Epistles by St. Paul), the *Katholikon* (Catholic Epistles) and the *Praxis* (Acts of the Apostles), and the Gospel proper to that day, if there are the books. If there are no books, then they shall read all what is appointed from the lessons of these books.
- A deacon shall not celebrate the liturgy, except that he shall read the Holy Gospel, unless a bishop be present and desire to

honor him. As regards to the rest of the lessons and the Gospel of the Morning Prayer, those of the priests who are present shall assist in the reading of them, and he who does not know how to read the Gospel shall not be allowed to officiate.

- As regards the deacons who have not officiated until now, none of them shall officiate until he reads well; but he shall study the writings and the Gospel of the Morning Prayer; and when he is skilled in reading and is proficient in what he reads, there shall be prepared for him a letter in which there shall be the signatures of a priest and of the chief of the priests, that he is already experienced in the reading of the books and then, it shall sent to the Cell (the bishop's residence), and it shall be signed, giving to him the permission to officiate. He shall take a rank in conformity with what is stated by the writings of the priests.
- The deacon who celebrates the liturgy shall not go away until he has finished communicating the people and dismissed them. Further, the priest shall communicate with him the *Despotikon* (alter utensil), and the priest shall raise the Chalice; and it is not allowed to him who officiates to raise the Chalice at all, until he has finished communicating the people.

- He who has not reached majority (adulthood) shall not carry the Chalice, lest some of it be spilled, and this is a great sin; but he shall carry it who has the ability to take care of it.

*Canon three:*

- It is mandatory to respect the eves of Sundays and Festivals, christenings, and crowning (weddings) in the churches when it comes to alcohol. Every priest who drinks intoxicating drinks at them shall not celebrate at all on the morning of that eve.

*Canon four:*

- Priests shall not at all be present at banquets or wedding feasts where there are jesting and amusements; but if a man invite them to be present with him, they must eat and drink with moderation and with psalmody, and depart in peace before there is any jesting at all. Whosoever takes a priest to his house to a banquet where there are musicians and players and associates him (the priest) with him in his sin, is under suspension together with him (the priest).

*Canon five:*

- The Liturgy shall not be celebrated until after the Altar has been covered with a cloth other than the covering, which is upon it, and when the Liturgy is finished, it shall be folded up and removed. Further, the pieces of cloth which are upon it shall not be separated from it.

*Canon six:*

- None of the priests shall go forward to read anything from the books, nor shall any of them go up to the altar without the *sticharion* (priest's vestment), and none of them shall communicate at the Altar with his head covered, and likewise, none of them shall pray with a priest or read the Gospel with his head covered.

*Canon seven:*

- The Liturgies of the Feasts are reserved for the priests in every church as follows:
- For the archpriest and the chief archdeacon in every church there shall be the Liturgies which are set forth as follows, Christmas, Epiphany, Palm Sunday, Holy Thursday, doing the liturgy of the water,[45] Easter, the third day of Easter, Ascension, the feast of the Disciples—the liturgy of the water.[46]

---

[45] Thursday of Holy Week has a liturgy of the water, and a normal liturgy.

[46] The Feast of the Apostles (July 12th) has a liturgy of the water, and a normal liturgy.

- For the second rank, the Eve of Christmas (except in the Church of Abu Sergius where it is reserved for the archdeacon), the second day of Christmas, the Eve of Epiphany, the second day of Epiphany, the Great Thursday at the Liturgy, the second day following Easter, the feast of the Disciples at the Liturgy, the Great Saturday, the third day of Christmas, and the third day of Epiphany.
- The gospels which are read at Easter are reserved for the chief priests according to their ranks in every church, and the six Sundays of the Fast are reserved for the chief priests in every church according to their rank. On the rest of the days the liturgy shall be performed by those who are not of the rank of chief priests.
- With regard to him who does not undertake the reading of the Gospel or who is late in attendance, he who is after him in rank shall celebrate instead of him.

*Canon eight:*

- The Liturgy shall not be celebrated without two candles around the Altar; either two small ones or two large ones according to whichever there may be.

### Canon nine:

- If the priests of Jerusalem[47] agree to mix with the priests of Abu Sergius;[48] each of them shall take the rank which is legally his, with love and peace during the Fast or otherwise. Then there will be no controversy. Otherwise, they shall bring him whom they have chosen to be appointed over them as priest in Jerusalem to celebrate with them. And if they remain without a priest, then they cannot officiate separately.
- May God the Exalted strengthen the love between them, and may peace abide with them, and may He deliver them from the Adversary Satan, and may He render my heart favorable towards them, and may He inform me of their news concerning that which is agreeable, if it so please God the Exalted; and praise be to God for ever and ever eternally.

---

[47] Jerusalem was in the Crusaders' hand at this point with Catholic clergy in charge while the Orthodox clergy were kicked out.
[48] Main church in Alexandria.

The conclusion of the second book (canon) of the father, the patriarch, Anba Gabriel. God grant to us the acceptance of his prayer. Amen.

### A. *The Laws of Inheritance*

Gabriel Laws of Inheritance are essentially a sermon with biblical references of where inheritance is involved. He makes it clear that Christians are not meant to be concerned about material possession, as such the apostles and the fathers of the Church didn't address the issue directly.

Further, he makes it clear, that inheritance is a civil issue, where laws vary according to the time, place, and the context. Nonetheless, due to differing opinion of judges and to "not product discord or harm in religion," Gabriel decided to extract from the bible all the verses and stories related to inheritance.

### *Canons:*

In the Name of the Father and of the Son and of the Holy Spirit, One God. A summary of the laws of Inheritance which is a collection from the Old and New Testaments by the saintly and chosen father Abba Gabriel known as Ibn Turayk.

It was said that the Christian religion is built on the renunciation of this temporary and perishable world and on the rejection of its worthless and decaying possessions. And in the striving toward the eternal and everlasting homes, being zealous for its lucrative and profitable goods, and upon guarding against its (the world's) vanities and the fear of falling into its traps, and of entering into them, according to the saying of the pure Gospel, "Do not lay up for yourselves treasures on earth, where moth and rust destroy and where thieves break in and steal; but lay up for yourselves treasures in heaven, where neither moth nor rust destroys and where thieves do not break in and steal (Matt. 6:19-20)."

As well as "therefore do not worry about tomorrow, for tomorrow will worry about its own things. Sufficient for the day is its own trouble (Matt. 6:34). As such it was not possible for the Apostles and the early Fathers to make laws and canons for what belongs exclusively to the possessions of the world and their treasures, and for what they left to their heirs, their equals (the Patriarchs/clergy).

Therefore, the laws of the time prevailed on what to do in such things, when to be strict and when to be lenient, as to not produce discord or harm in the religion. The rulers began to look into the inheritances of the faithful according to their countries and the laws of their times, with their power extended depending on their condition and ability to settle those issues. They did not agree in one opinion and did not follow in their judgments arguments in which they could find support and a basis, but each of them says: I am a canon of my time, and this was made according to the degree of my knowledge and my understanding.

It often happens that the pronouncements of the judges on one matter are different and opposed to that which is right by reason of the lapse of time. So, I deemed it good to extract whatever is found in the Holy Scriptures in reference to these inheritances, and to write these down, and to establish an authority both to be a support and to be relied upon in matters wherein I judge. In God I trust, and by Him I am directed, and in Him I confide.

The Divine Scriptures contain about these references about inheritance; Adam begat Seth, and Seth begat Enosh, Then one came after the other until they reached the Flood which was in the time of Noah. Then we say that Noah begat Shem, and Shem, begat Arphaxad, that Abraham begat Isaac, and Isaac begat Jacob and thus it is evident that each one of them inherited from his father.

Then we say that Jacob begat twelve sons, and he blessed Ephraim and Manasseh and made both of them as Reuben and Simeon his two sons in honor of Joseph his son, and that his successors inherit the promised land.

This is a proof that two sons inherit from their father, for when Sarah bore Isaac and had weaned him, she saw that Ishmael and Hagar mocked him, and she said to Abraham "'Cast out this bondwoman and her son; for the son of this bondwoman shall not be heir with my son, namely with Isaac'"(Gen. 21:10). And this was grievous for Abraham, and God said to Abraham, "Do not let it be displeasing in your sight because of the lad or because of your bondwoman. Whatever Sarah has said to you, listen to her voice; for in Isaac your seed shall be called (Gen. 21:12).

The Fourth Book (Numbers) in the twelfth section of the Law (Torah) contains how the daughters of Zelophehad, the son of Ham, the son of Galaad, the son of Manasseh, of the tribe of Manasseh, the son of Joseph, approached and stood before Moses and Eleazar, the priest and before the chiefs and all the congregation, at the door of the tabernacle, and they said:

> "'Our father died in the wilderness; but he was not in the company of those who gathered together against the Lord, in company with Korah, but he died in his own sin; and he had no sons. Why should the name of our father be removed from among his family because he had no son? Give us a possession among our father's brothers.' So, Moses brought

their case before the Lord. And the Lord spoke to Moses, saying: 'The daughters of Zelophehad speak what is right; you shall surely give them a possession of inheritance among their father's brothers, and cause the inheritance of their father to pass to them. And you shall speak to the children of Israel, saying: 'If a man dies and has no son, then you shall cause his inheritance to pass to his daughter. If he has no daughter, then you shall give his inheritance to his brothers. If he has no brothers, then you shall give his inheritance to his father's brothers. And if his father has no brothers, then you shall give his inheritance to the relative closest to him in his family, and he shall possess it. And it shall be to the children of Israel a statute of judgment, just as the Lord commanded Moses'" (Num. 27:3-11).

Further, the Holy Gospel says, "A certain man had two sons. And the younger of them said to his father, 'Father, give me the portion of goods that falls to me.' So he divided to them his livelihood ( Luke 15:11-12). And, it (the Gospel) says in another place, "Then one from the crowd said to Him, "Teacher, tell my brother to divide the inheritance with me. But He said to him, 'Man, who made Me a judge or an arbitrator over you?' And He said to them, 'Take heed and beware of covetousness, for one's life does not consist in the abundance of the things he possesses (Luke 12:13-14).'"

The *Didascalia*[49] says: "Give unto the orphans the substance of their fathers, and to the widows, the substance of their husbands."

As regards to Constantine,[50] he says:

> "Inheritance is according to classes and orders; and the first order in the inheritance is, that if a man die without having written a will and leaves behind male and female children, they shall inherit equally. And if he have written a will, then his son shall inherit as he desired, and if he wish to give any of his substance in alms, let him give a fourth part of it in alms. And if he dies suddenly, and if he have no son, and if he have not written a will, then his father, if he be alive, shall be his heir; and if his father be not alive, then his mother and his brothers shall

---

[49] *Didascalia Apostolorum*, or *Didascalia*, is a Christian treatise composed in Antioch, probably from the third century modeled after the *Didache*.

[50] Constantine the Great, the first Christian emperor of Rome. Laws here probably refer to Roman law in general, than to Constantine himself.

be his heirs. The mother (shall receive) the same portion as each of her children. And if none of these survive, then his paternal uncles shall be his heirs, and if he have no paternal uncles, then his sister's son shall be his heir, and if he have no nephew (son of his sister), then his paternal aunt and her children both male and female shall be the heirs. Whoever is nearest to him in consanguinity shall be the heir."

The book of Job says, "he made his daughters heirs with his male children (Job 42:15)." According to the Epistle of Paul to the Corinthians the Second, in the ninth section,[51] "For the children ought not to lay up for the parents, but the parents for the children" (2 Cor. 12:14).

What is allowed to be done with inheritances after the deceased's intentions about alms has been made known, is that which is spent on the needy and the churches, and the requirements of the dead, such as the shroud and the coffin, and finally the bearers and gravediggers, as is written in both the *Didascalia* and the Ecclesiastical Canons.

If a man dies and leaves behind male and female children. his children (shall divide) the

---

[51] Probably different way to organize the epistle, the verse is in Chapter 12.

inheritance equally between them according to the rule of the first law. And if he had a wife, and she had from him male and female children, then she shall have the same as each of them; according to the saying of the Holy Gospel: "the two shall be one flesh, and both of them are not two but one flesh" (Matt. 19:5-6).

The *Didascalia* says: "Give the substance of the orphans to the orphans, and the substance of the widows to the widows; for it is of the substance of their husbands." Peter says in the *Katholikon*: "Husbands, likewise, dwell with them with understanding, giving honor to the wife, as to the weaker vessel, and as being heirs together of the grace of life" (1 Pet. 3:7).

And whoever has a wife and has no children by her, if he die and have no relatives, then she shall have whatsoever he leave behind: and as regards the remainder of the family and relatives, they shall not inherit at all with the children. And if she has no children or he (the deceased) have an heir other than her, then she shall have half of the inheritance, and the other half (shall go) to the heirs. And the degrees of the heirs are according to this rule: The father excludes others from the inheritance, the mother and brothers receive equally together or alone; then the paternal uncle, then the sister's son, then the aunt and female children.

From the Canons of the Kings, the 88th Section: 'If a man die without having made a will and leave behind an only son or an only daughter, and afterwards the son and the daughter die, and his mother be alive, and if he have paternal uncles and nephews (sons of paternal uncles), they shall have a third of his inheritance, and they shall divide it equally, and two thirds (shall go) to his mother."

The inheritance shall cease to be given to the women after the first degree, and they shall not inherit with the males, that is to say, neither the children of sisters, nor the children of paternal aunts, nor the children of maternal aunts, nor the children of their daughters shall inherit; that is to say, the children of the daughters shall not inherit with the children of the male children.

if the father have no male descendants, then his tribe shall inherit from the female (children), and after the descendants of the father, then the descendants of the mother of the man shall inherit, and relationship shall exclude those who are distant relatives, and near relatives shall inherit; and the son of a son (grandson) shall not inherit with the son, but he shall inherit with the wife, and he shall not inherit with the sons and the brothers.

Praise be to God for ever and ever. Completed is what was found of the Canons which are attributed to the lord patriarch Gabriel. God grant to us his prayers. Amen.

## Part 4. Saif al-Islam[52]

After the assassination of the Caliph Al-Amir Bi-Ahkam Allah, a prolonged succession crisis took place. A distant cousin named Al-Hafiz eventually managed to ascend the throne despite being contested and challenged by many factions. At some point in his early reign, several high-ranking Coptic government officials were dismissed and replaced with a group of *Al-Asharaf,* rich Sunni men with claimed heritage to the prophet. Additionally, the sons of the Caliph, fearful of another powerful vizier that could sideline them, urged their father to not have a vizier from the outside and keep the day-to-day administration within the family.

As such, the oldest son was entrusted with the vizierate and to run the government. This arrangement only lasted two months as the vizier died suddenly, most likely from natural causes. Again so, another son was appointed. But he too, did not last for long. The Armenian cohort of the army, now feeling threatened and isolated, staged a coup. They elevated the youngest of the three sons, a certain Hasan, to the post of vizier against the wishes of the Caliph and his older brother.

The coup's execution was lacking, and it quickly turned into a brief civil war between the

---

[52] Literally, the sword of Islam.

Caliph, his middle son, and the Muslim Nubian cohort of the army that supported them versus the younger son, Hasan and the Armenian cohort. Nonetheless, the Armenian cohort gained an upper hand quickly and al Hafiz capitulated to their demands, appointing Hasan as the vizier and the effective ruler of Egypt.

Rather than being the start of a new stable regime, the new vizier was—to put it mildly—unfit for office. He proved to be an overly harsh official with little experience and absolutely no interest in surrounding himself with good counsel. In less than a year, he turned on the Armenian cohort that brought him to power, started executing his own people for both real and perceived insults, and finally, his preferred method of fundraising was to confiscate and fine the state elite. As part of that cycle of arrests and fines, he imprisoned the Patriarch Gabriel and ransomed him for 1,000 denars.

And so, having successfully ridded themselves of the old vizier, the same Armenian cohort of the army decided to get rid of the new vizier only 10 months after they had elevated him to power. A new vizier was needed though, and as Hasan was the last of the Caliph's adult sons, their plan was in danger of backfiring spectacularly if they did not have a solid candidate of their own.

Over in the Delta, there was an exceptional candidate for the office named Bahram. An experienced and beloved Armenian governor who was in the mold of Badr al Jamali, only with a lot more charisma and a lot less need for underhanded ruthlessness. He had the charms and the personality to win him a loyal following without resorting to excessive violence. There was one problem though: that governor was a Christian, and not a nominal one that could be persuaded to convert or even pretend to convert. He was none other than the brother of the Armenian Patriarch, Gregory, with a long family history that saw his family ruling Antioch itself on behalf of the Byzantines at some point.

As such, his links to Christianity was too deep for pious Muslims who were already anxious about the continued Crusader expansion. The reality was that by far, he was the best qualified man for the job, both as an experienced politician and as a competent general tailor-made for the times. Before coming to Egypt, Bahram was an Armenian prince for a small territory of land stuck between the Crusaders and Turkish tribes.

There, after a lot of fighting and trying to eke out a peaceful but independent existence between them, Bahram was pushed out under obscure circumstances to seek his fortunes in Egypt, where Badr and then his son were well-disposed toward Armenians and often sponsored them. In essence, he was trusted by the army as one of them and at the same time considered enough of an outsider that he could be relied on to stay loyal to the Caliph. So, there was hope that he could overcome that resistance against a Christian becoming the vizier. As such, in the middle of the army rebellion against Hasan, Bahram was persuaded to come to Cairo from the Western Delta where he was staying as a governor.

His timing was perfect, as while he was on the way, the palace was surrounded with rebellious troops asking for the head of Hasan. A request that was granted when, in an almost Shakespearean fashion, al-Hafiz asked his son to willingly drink poison and die peacefully whereby his death, the kingdom and his father's throne would be saved. That's how one Coptic source put it anyway, the truth might not be as dramatic, as the Muslim sources just say that he was poisoned by the Caliph's physician.

Regardless, Bahram's arrival at this point where he was the only viable choice to succeed the Caliph's son, and at the same time taking no part of his murder made his appointment to the vizierate almost automatic. As both al-Hafiz worried about his own life and the army worried about a population backlash, welcomed the Armenian governor as a savior.

As a measure of his standing with the army and the expectation, he was given the honorific title "Saif al-Islam" or the "sword of Islam" by the Caliph. This was a fascinating period, given that imams were preaching across the palace about dhimmitude[53] and all the limitations that non-Muslims were supposed to abide by, yet here stood the most powerful man of the land, a dhimmi himself. The only man who could save the Fatimids from themselves and the infidel Crusaders—was an infidel himself.

As one would expect, throughout the short two years that Bahram was around, the Caliph was under a lot of pressure to dismiss him. Most of the noise came from a religiously zealous mob and the local imams, but they posed no serious danger on their own. The real threat to the palace was *Al-Asharaf*, the Sunni nobility who put their resources behind mobilizing that mob dangerously. Like Badr before him, Bahram strongly encouraged and sponsored Armenians to come and settle in Egypt to take administrative positions as well as serve in the army. However, unlike in Badr's time, lots of Armenians under immense pressure from the

---

[53] A controversial term used to describe the situation of non-Muslims living in Muslim lands, where non-Muslims are free to practice their religion, provided they observe certain restrictions. This particular term was coined to denote that non-Muslims cannot bear arms and must therefore rely on Muslim soldiers for protection.

Crusaders and Turkish tribes welcomed the call to resettle in Egypt. According to Islamic sources, 30,000 Armenians relocated to Egypt in less than a year. This migration induced absolute paranoia and panic in the Egyptian Muslim ruling nobility who feared a Christian takeover and imbalanced population dynamic with native Copts and Armenian immigrants. As Leila al-Imad put it, in her "The Fatimid Vizierate" book,

> "The mood that swept the Caliphate was paranoia; anyone who was not a Muslim or from the established Egyptian aristocracy was suspect."[54]

One of the members of this nobility, Ridwan ibn Walakhshi, fanned the flame of religious war and rebelled against the palace on strict lines of defending Islam against the Christians. Along with local imams all over Egypt, he called for a "Jihad against the infidels," who were their next-door neighbors at this point.

Ridwan instructed his men to raise the Qur'an as their standard, literally attaching the books to their lances, putting any Muslim that opposed them or attempts a reasonable discussion in a very uncomfortable position. After all, how can they fight men who have the Qu'ran in their spears?

---

[54] Leila al-Imad, *The Fatimid Vizierate 969-1172,* (Oakland: University of California Press, 2007), 114.

Shall they desecrate the holy book? Even the Caliph who absolutely hated Ridwan and had grown to like Bahram by this point could do nothing as civil war was about to engulf his kingdom.

In Cairo, despite the rhetoric of holy war, a significant cohort of the army continued to be loyal to Bahram and, unlike the men that Ridwan gathered, they were much better trained and equipped. But with jihad called against him, Bahram would have to essentially march town to town burning everything to the ground. The only way he could be king was to be the king of ashes, and so he did the unthinkable: he told the army to stand down and not fight back.

*The History of the Patriarchs* records his speech to the army. This is probably not a literal word-for-word transcription, but maybe sufficient to give us a window to his motivation and reasoning.

> "[if we fight] without fail I shall die and God will require of me the blood of the slain from among you and from among them. The kingdom of this land God has given to the Muslims, and it is not lawful nor permissible for me by God to fight against the people for their kingdom, and to deprive them of their rights. Had the Caliph not asked aid of me for what happened to him from his son, and agreed with me about what I

did in his service and his obedience, I would not have begun anything of myself. Arise, take what you are able of your money and your children. And let us go to Qus, to take my brother. Then we will go to our country and leave to the people their kingdom; there is no need for us to make war against them."

Basically, Bahram concluded that fighting a religious war would lead to an unwinnable generational war and he had no interest in pursuing such a thing. So, he decided to leave Egypt and go somewhere else. As expected, not all of his soldiers agreed, with a significant portion intending to stay and defend their new homes in Egypt. As such, the army was split. Some followed Bahram to upper Egypt, and some decided to stay with their families and children in Cairo. Also, for context, Bahram had two brothers: the Patriarch Gregory—who was dead at this point and replaced by a man named Ananias who was operating in Cairo—and the governor of Qus, a wealthy city in upper Egypt with a sizable Christian population.

Unfortunately for Bahram and his brother, his desire to avoid bloodshed and holy wars was out of fashion. The Muslims inhabitants of Qus had heard about Ridwan's rebellion and already lynched Bahram's brother as well as any Christian they could find. As such, by the time Bahram made it to

Qus—it was too late, his brother was dead with his family. He was briefly anguished about the loss and besieged the city to punish its inhabitants, but quickly accepted the tragedy and abandoned the siege. His troops were instructed to disburse and look out for themselves.

Meanwhile, Bahram himself took refuge in the White Monastery,[55] a famous and venerable site established by Shenouda the Archimandrite more than 600 years earlier. There, he hoped to be able to finish whatever he had left in his life in peace living as a simple monk.

In Cairo, the situation played out in a similar fashion. When Ridwan arrived, the population opened the gates to him, and the army basically disappeared. Then, a massacre of the Christians occurred with the Armenian quarter being specifically targeted.

> "[Ridwan] plundered the churches of Cairo and the Khandak, and the Muslims burned the dwellings of the Armenians known as Az-Zuhri, and they killed their patriarch and all whom they found with him of the monks in the monastery."[56]

---

[55] The White Monastery survives to the present day near Sohag, Egypt. It is a functioning monastery, open for visitors and monks.
[56] *History of the Patriarchs* 3.1, 50.

The patriarch here—is the Patriarch of the Armenians. With his death and the massacre, the Armenian's presence in Cairo was extinguished, at least in the sense of a cohesive ethnic unit with political power. Those who survived the massacre had to find somewhere else to live or assimilate. There would still be Armenians in Egypt, and a new Patriarch would even be eventually consecrated with the help of Gabriel, but their presence would never be the same.

As one would expect while all of this was going on, everyday life for Copts and the Patriarch Gabriel was extremely difficult. This became especially even more so after Ridwan was established in the Vizierate and started enforcing dhimmitude to its fullest extent. First, he ordered that no Christian should be employed in the government, essentially firing most of the scribes and bookkeepers of the administration. This caused economic and logistical problems, so it was quickly remodified to a policy of removing Christians from important posts rather than from all posts.

Second, the Gizya, the Poll tax on non-Muslims, was increased dramatically and enforced zealously. The rich paid 4.6 denars, the middle class paid 2 and change, and most paid about 1.5 denars. Even landless peasants and beggars had to pay something for the symbolism of it as downtrodden others only living due to the mercy of their rulers. That symbolic Gizya ended up being a *dirham*—a silver coin. Naturally, all of the dress restrictions and other miscellaneous restrictions that Christians and Jews had to abide by were also strictly enforced. In the middle of all of this, or perhaps because of it, as chaos reigned and agriculture was neglected, a severe famine hit Egypt in AD 1139/1140.

The famine made one neighbor turn against another and an even greater cycle of persecution took place. Mobs would descend on churches, destroy them and turn it into mosques. Likewise, monasteries were rumored to contain magic and treasures and were raided by a combination of fortune seekers and angry mobs. Several monks were also tried for witchcraft in a ridiculous spectacle meant to humiliate them publicly.

Now, the greatness of Gabriel is that while these events would have broken or at least diminished the achievements of many Patriarchs, his zeal for reform persevered even as the act of surviving in of itself was enough. He fought one battle after another for his vision of reformation.

First when John, son of Sanhut died in AD 1134—Gabriel finally abolished the diocese of Cairo altogether. He asserted the right of the Patriarch to operate from there, the heart of government. Then, he forbade the common but disturbing act of burying the pious inside the churches, going as far as exhuming previous Patriarchs from churches. When he was ignored and people buried a beloved priest there anyways, he closed the church until they understood the seriousness of his decree.

He strictly enforced the no simony rule and suspended bishops and clergy who skirted it one way or another. This made him quite unpopular fora brief period of time among some bishops who considered it to be heavy handed enforcement. Nonetheless, he concentrated some fifty-three bishops—possibly doubling the number that was already there—and so, those who opposed him were a dwindling minority from a group that was increasingly being shaped into his own image.

We are told, as an example of his efforts against simony, how a priest from a wealthy family tried to buy a diocese from the Patriarch early in his reign. Naturally, Gabriel refused. Regardless, the priest wasn't necessarily a terrible choice for that diocese as he was learned and pious enough, but the simony offer essentially shut the door for him ever becoming a bishop. Unfortunately, as was the habit, instead of the money going to the Patriarchate as simony, it went as a bribe for a palace official to pressure Gabriel into making the priest a bishop. Gabriel stood his ground and fought it all the way to al Hafiz himself, who took the Patriarch's side and let him manage the affairs of the church as he saw fit.

This was all before Ridwan took power and increased pressure on Christians. Once the cycle of persecution started, it became clear that the priest might convert to Islam and would cause a lot more damage to satisfy his grudge against Gabriel. So, the Patriarch ended up ordaining him a bishop to prevent his conversion. The simony money that the priest "donated" for the office went that very same day to renovate a monastery, never touching the Patriarch's hands who truly considered it a great sin.

Similarly to the story of that priest, a monk from a rich family ended up holding a grudge against Gabriel for not taking his monetary contribution into consideration when dealing with him. Unlike the priest however, he did end up converting which ached at the heart of the Patriarch who took it as a personal failure. As his biographer puts it,

> "this affair was hard to bear for the father, the patriarch, and he repented of it with bitter repentance; and after it he did not repeat being severe with anyone, fearing lest others might do the same."[57]

---

[57] *History of the Patriarchs* 3.1, 56.

Even on the political stage, Gabriel was quite impressive. As Egypt became weaker politically, the Ethiopian king wanted to be able to ordain Ethiopian bishops rather than depend on whoever was sent from Egypt. Naturally, the request was sent to the vizier as well as the Patriarch—with probably gifts to nudge the palace to push Gabriel to do it. But Gabriel staunchly opposed the idea and explained to the palace that ordaining more bishops or allowing native Ethiopian bishops would more than likely mean the complete independence of the Ethiopian church from Egypt. This, in turn, would cause a loss of leverage between the two states and potentially a hostile relationship. The palace agreed, and no bishops were ordained[58].

Gabriel's greatest achievement is how he handled two practical problems of his day: the physical and spiritual food for his flock. First, for the physical food, the famine and instability beginning at Ridwan's reign had the potential for a lot of misery if it were not for Gabriel. Although the details are murky, it seems that Gabriel last 5 years, where famine and unrest was the greatest—he put all of his intellectual and administrative might

---

[58] To be clear here, while not ordaining Ethiopian bishops was clearly better for Egypt politically, it was not an ideal situation for the state of the Ethiopian church. There was a constant need for native bishops who knew the land and the people and could serve as able stewards.

making sure people didn't starve to death, quite literally building a supply chain of grain across Egypt.

The second, the spiritual food, was his effort to stamp out several strange traditions that were taking hold among the everyday Copts. For example, a monk claimed that he could see the future, and even offered his services to Bahram. But the vizier found him "diseased in his intellect" sending him away. Gabriel had no tolerance for such things and through his written cannons and verbal exhortation made sure no monk could play the magician without serious threats of excommunication. Similarly, he outlawed a strange feast of the Archangel Michael that involved animal sacrifice and riffed too close to pagan rituals.

Even among the elite, Gabriel constantly exhorted them about the issue of concubines despite their constant threat to convert to Islam if Gabriel pushed them too far. In a way, Gabriel was all that one could ask for in a pope, encapsulating the spirit of a warrior fighting different battles day in and day out. Still, the progress he made while he was alive was extremely limited due to being constantly besieged with difficult obstacles to overcome.

As Swanson put it,

> "Gabriel found himself charged to shepherd an under-catechized Church, full of people who were naturally religious but who lacked the basic Christian formation necessary to sort out traditional church teaching from heresy, or Christian sense from nonsense. Perhaps many of them, almost by a process of osmosis, were becoming socialized into the religious language of the mosque."[59]

And so, like a wave shaping a rock, he battled again and again until the day he died in AD 1145, ultimately, leaving contributions that we today—900 years later—can appreciate as a bright spot of reform in a long and dark tunnel.

---

[59] Mark N. Swanson, *The Coptic Papacy in Islamic Egypt 641-1517*, (Cairo: American University of Cairo Press, 2010), 73.

# CHAPTER IV

## The Context of the Canons

A non-Coptic historian once wrote that:

"The civilization of medieval Egypt was essentially Arab and Muslim with no tangible Christian component, and with each century it became more so. Even those Copts who were not ready to abandon their own faith gradually adopted Arabic as their sole language. And together with Arabic they took over many of the profoundly Islamic values that were implicit in the language of the Qur'an. The furtive reminiscences of Coptic history were integrated into Muslim writing, remolded and arrayed as forebodings of Islam Triumphant, and thus lost their character as tokens of an alternative civilization."[60]

In essence, proclaiming that during the very period of these canons, as Arabic was becoming the sole language of the Copts, Coptic civilization ceased to exist; the agency and the identity of the Copts as a people was no longer there. This book attempts to portray this period as a period of transition rather than complete erasure. The Copts did not lose their character as "tokens of an alternative civilization;" rather, they adapted to the

---

[60] Ulrich Haarmann, "Regional Sentiment in Medieval Islamic Egypt," *Bulletin of the School of Oriental and African Studies* 43, no. 1 (1980): 55.

changing circumstances to keep their sense of identity and group dynamic alive.

Christodoulous navigated the political reality of Cairo as the center of Egypt and moved the seat of the church there. Yet, he himself stayed away. Badr al Jamali resuscitated the dying Fatimids, but also invited the Armenian Patriarch to establish an Armenian church in Egypt. Cyril cooperated when asked to ordain a metropolitan picked by the government for Ethiopia, but stone-walled a project to insert the state between the clergy and the people.

Moreover, even in the times of Michael and Macarius where the tension between the Coptic civil elite in Cairo and the Patriarchate was palatable, a Christian Armenian ruled the land. Finally, with Gabriel, the complementary forces of transition are in full view. He tells his clergy to teach their children Coptic, while in the very same breath tells them to instruct the faithful to know the basic prayers of the church in Arabic so that they could understand their prayers.

Indeed, with each passing century, the Coptic identity was not being erased, rather solidified and built around a Coptic church with Arabic as its spoken language.[61] Medieval Copts

---

[61] At least up until the 20th century and the migration out of Egypt which is yet again, reshaping that identity.

were not bystanders of history, but actively participated in the formation of their own identity and the identity of the Copts to this day.

The difficulty in studying this period often means that it is skipped over altogether in the story of the Copts. There is the apostle Mark, then the great persecution, followed by the monastic movement and the great Patriarchs Athanasius, Cyril, and Dioscorus—then comes Islam; for many, the Coptic story ends there.

The facts are, as of the writing on this book, when the Copts fast, celebrate a feast, attend a liturgy, or even pray—they are much closer to the world and the traditions of Gabriel and Christodoulos than they are to Athanasius and Dioscorus.

After Gabriel, another period of intense transformation took place where it was no longer minor canons and small theological treatises being produced by Patriarchs. Rather, a golden age of Copto-Arabic literature with many actors, both laymen and clergy. There was Awlad al-'Assal, a group of brothers that produced comprehensive canons for the church, extensive theological treatises, as well as a Coptic dictionary and a grammar book.

Then there was Abu Shakir Ibn al-Rahib, whose father was the tutor of Awlad al-A'assal. He wrote an extensive treatise on the divinity and humanity of Christ, a survey of the ecumenical councils, a Coptic grammar book, and a few other entries.

Lastly, coming a generation later and marking the end of this period was a certain Ibn Kabar. He wrote an encyclopedia of Coptic religious knowledge and traditions in twenty-four sections with numerous supplements. This encyclopedia is undoubtedly the most comprehensive record of Coptic culture and laws that meticulously discusses every detail imaginable concerning the church with a collection of equally impressive volumes—six in total with topics ranging from apologetics to Coptic grammar.

One might argue that this period represented not the death of Coptic culture, but rather the peak. Between the late-Fatimids and the Ayyubids periods in Egypt, the Copts produced an encyclopedia, a world history, a Copto-Arabic dictionary, a law code, full bible commentaries, massive tomes of theological treatises, and an Arabic translation of the Bible.

Further, unlike the other golden ages for the Copts, like the time of Athanasius and Cyril, or the latter half of the 20th Century, this cultural flourishing was not driven by a strong Patriarchate or favorable social circumstances. Rather, this was a golden age that was not supposed to happen, a brief light in a period of famine, absent leadership, and multiple Crusades.

To end, we must remember that identities are a fluid abstraction that is constantly evolving and changing. Yet, there are moments of history that are unique to examine the complexity of identity—moments of transition where a collective culture starts to adapt to difficult circumstances. The period between Christodoulos and Gabriel is one of those powerful moments, where the Coptic identity took a significant turn and ensured its survival as a civilization.

# Bibliography

al-Imad, Leila S. *The Fatimid Vizierate, 969-1172.* Berlin: K. Schwarz, 1990.

Burmester, O. H. E. "The Canons of Christodoulos, Patriarch of Alexandria (A.D. 1047-1077)." *Le Muséon* 45 (1932): 51-84.

Burmester, O. H. E. "The Canons of Cyril II, LXVII Patriarch of Alexandria." *Le Muséon* 49 (1936): 245-288.

Burmester, O. H. E. "The Canons of Gabriel Ibn Turaik, LXX Patriarch of Alexandria." *Le Muséon* 46 (1933): 43-54.

Brett, M. *The Fatimid Empire*. Edinburgh: Edinburgh University Press, 2017.

Kennedy, Hugh. *The Prophet and the Age of the Caliphates: the Islamic Near East from the Sixth to the Eleventh Century*. London: Longman Publishing, 1986.

Swanson, Mark N. *The Coptic Papacy in Islamic Egypt (641-1517)*. Cairo: The American University in Cairo Press, 2010.

Sawius Ibn al-Mukkafa'. *History of the Patriarchs of*
 the Egyptian Church Volume 2, Part 3. Atiya, A. S. Abd al-Masih, Y. Burmester, O.H.E., editors and translators. Cairo: Publications de la Société d'Archéologie Copte, 1959.

Sawirus Ibn al-Mukaffa'. *The History of the Patriarchs of the Egyptian Church* Volume 3, Part 1. Khater, A. O.H.E.-Burmester, O.H.E., editors and translators. Cairo: Publications de la Société d'Archéologie Copte, 1968.

Walker, Paul E. "The Isma'ili Da'wa and the Fatimid Caliphate," in The Cambridge History of Egypt, i,
 120-50.

# About the Author

Jonathan Adly is a pharmacist and an entrepreneur whose activities span many different worlds. In 2017, he founded and produced *The History of the Copts* podcast, the first narrative history of the Copts in audio format. He then went on to be part of the Coptic Voice founding team and a board member. Born in Egypt, he emigrated to the United States with his family in 2003. He has a PharmD with post-doctoral residency training from Long Island University, and MBA in Marketing from Wilmington University. He worked for many years as a Clinical Pharmacist and a hospital administrator, founding a few companies along the way.

www.ingramcontent.com/pod-product-compliance
Lightning Source LLC
Chambersburg PA
CBHW061801070526
44586CB00023B/2656